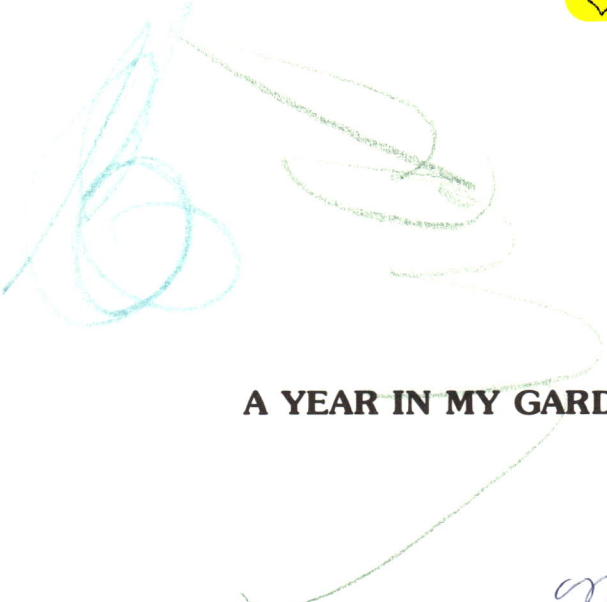

A YEAR IN MY GARDEN

Sittu

David

339-8578

Kathryn Beth

359 - 1915

Super @reshole

*

*

A YEAR IN
MY GARDEN

ANGELA DENEVI

Illustrations by the Author

GREAT BASIN PRESS • **RENO**

Portions of this book which originally
appeared in the author's newspaper
column, "Come Into My Garden," are
reprinted by permission of the Reno
Gazette-Journal.

The plant list in Appendix I was
originally compiled by the author for
Bill Carlos, Washoe County Cooperative
Extension Agent.

Portions of this book previously appeared
in an earlier work by Angela DeNevi,
Come Into My Garden (Sparks, Nevada:
Dave's Printing & Publishing, 1973).

GREAT BASIN PRESS

Box 11162, Reno, Nevada   89510

Printed in the United States of America

This book is dedicated to all those gardeners who, through their hard work and perseverance, have proved that our lovely desert valley can be made more beautiful because of their efforts.

CONTENTS

FOREWORD

If you live in the Reno-northwestern Nevada area and are a gardener or have any interest in landscaping, you will find this a very useful book. You may ask - why? Because the author has the answers to what, where and how to plant flowers, shrubs and trees.

My longtime friend, Angela DeNevi, graduated from the Sutro, Nevada, Grammar School and Dayton High School. In 1933, she completed work on a Bachelor of Science degree in biology at the University of Nevada. After teaching in the Washoe County Schools for many years, she retired and purchased an acre of land on Boxer Drive in Reno. This space gave her the ideal exposure for her garden.

She has fruit trees, irises, peonies, roses - everything and anything that blooms or bears fruit in the Reno area. Her knowledge of the plants acclimated to our area has expanded into garden club lectures, programs and her newspaper column. In 1971, her column "Come Into My Garden" began and it still appears in the *Reno Gazette-Journal*.

If you have a love for gardening, come into Angela's garden.

Louie A. Gardella
Reno

March 1989

PREFACE

This book was written for those who live in that area of northwestern Nevada east of the Sierra foothills – that arid, upland portion where the winds blow cold in winter and hot and dry in summer. It is for the gardeners who know nights when the thermometer drops below freezing only to awaken to a sunny day that laughs as if it were all a joke.

Those of us who know this climate learn to take it in our stride and that we must protect our precious plants from these sudden changes. Through our efforts they survive and greet each coming year as the seasons advance.

Long ago as a beauty-starved youngster, I carried water in a pail to some poor, struggling little plants that contended with the blistering hot sun and the rocky soil of a mining town. I had little knowledge of their needs. Today the situation has changed. A half acre set in an ideal location on the side of a hill receives the first rays of the morning sun and the last ones at night. Good soil and plenty of water make it easy to grow things. Extensive reading and experience have brought me rewards and the knowledge which I once lacked.

My garden is not neatly arranged and kept just so. It is very informal and contains specimens of almost every plant that can be grown in our environment. At one time or another different plants dominate the scene depending on my fancy at the moment. A half acre can hold only so much and some plants must give way to others for a while.

I am not a professionally trained gardener. If I can raise these plants, so can you. Follow the suggestions given, and do not try to cross

Mother Nature. Do a little at a time and become
familiar with each new specimen you plant.
Whether you are an actual gardener or the armchair variety, I hope you will find something of
interest when you come into my garden.

December 1988

A YEAR IN MY GARDEN

INTRODUCTION: SEASONS' KALEIDOSCOPE

Spring's harbingers come early to our area as the first snowdrops push their venturesome noses out in February. They are followed by the crocuses which brighten March with clumps of yellow, white, purple and variegated hues.

But it is April with its snappy breezes, brisk, sunny days interspersed with showers, and gusts of wind that really gets the season off to a good start. From my hillside site one can see the surrounding countryside take on a faint tinge of green as the fields awaken to new life. Leafless trees that top many of the roofs of the city are beginning to show traces of tiny leaves. Birds fly here and there picking seeds that have dropped from weeds of the preceding year.

In the gardens, drifts of hyacinths, narcissus, daffodils and early tulips make us all aware that Nature is breaking forth in another display of beauty. Violets spring up overnight and the smaller bulbs cluster under shrubs and among the crevices in the rock gardens that will later be covered with all types of small flora.

May follows with the later tulips – Darwins, parrots, cottage types, and the lily-flowered. The lupines send up spears of many colors. Delphiniums stand tall in the background echoing the rainbow tones of the iris beds. Flamboyant Oriental poppies, no longer limited to a brilliant orange flame, range from white through the pinks, from the very dainty pastels to the brilliant shocking tones, the deep rose shades and the glamorous bi-colors, with here and there a rich, deep red and a maroon that is almost black.

In May the garden clubs of the Reno-Sparks area get together to put on a spring flower

show in Reno, in which younger gardeners, as
well as those of many years experience, bring
their flowers to display for the pleasure of the
general public. Flower arrangers parade their
talent, and the grower of the unusual specimen
awakens the interest of the audience to something
different.

June, the month of brides and early
summer beauty, puts on its rose display. From
the private gardens of individuals to the Municipal
Rose Garden in Idlewild Park, our area displays
a spectacle of blooms that is equal to the best.

Summer's heat, though it slows the work
of many gardeners, fills the perennial beds with
many varieties and colors that carry on bravely.
Proper watering and the cool of the nights give
gardens the vigor to withstand the heat of another
day. Even the weeds that plagued us so badly in
the early spring days relax in their campaign to
take over the flower beds. The onslaught of crabgrass and broadleaf weeds can be controlled by
proper measures and the gardener can relax a
little at this time.

September brings the first killing frost
followed by Indian Summer that lasts through October and into November. At this time the lovely
chrysanthemums take their place in the ever-
changing kaleidoscope that brings the garden
season to a close. As the year comes to an end,
the pyracanthas, holly bushes and other small
fruited shrubs and trees supply banquets for the
birds that winter over in our yards.

Again the leaves fly, the wind blows, the
snow falls, and the land seems to fall into a deep
slumber. For two months the outdoor work is at
a standstill. We study our new garden catalogs,
and even as we do that, the first snowdrop peeping out from under the junipers tells us that
another spring is on its way.

1. GETTING STARTED

Do you remember how many times you promised yourself that this was the year you were going to do things with your garden? Not until late June did you realize that you had gotten nowhere with your many plans. Then you had satisfied yourself with a few plants here and there.

What about really doing something this year? The secret of a successful, soul-satisfying garden is a manageable goal. Whatever it is – houseplants, a new perennial bed, basic landscaping in a new lot, or a rose garden – fix your goal in mind and prepare yourself to go at it systematically. Don't plan to do everything in one season. Lay your foundation carefully and your work will be half done. Rome was not built in a day, and neither will your garden be done in one weekend. Start early with your planning and set a goal for each working day.

Adequate tools are a must, and you should have at least the following for outdoor work:

- A large spade – for deep digging
- A small spade – to turn the soil over
- A bamboo rake – to clean up debris
- A strong metal rake – to level the soil
- A weed digger – to remove long-rooted perennial weeds
- Trowels – for transplanting and working flower beds
- Pruning shears – for delicate trimming
- Lopping shears – for heavier material

Other useful tools include:

- A small wheel barrow
- A scuffle hoe
- Gloves and knee pads

Of course, you may find that you need other tools, but those mentioned should do almost everything. Plan a place to keep your tools so you won't have to spend valuable time looking for them.

Plans should be made to acquire supplies to eliminate those insects that are a nightmare to every gardener. I use few pesticides, limiting myself to two or three of the least toxic. Soapsuds do wonders in discouraging aphids and other sucking and chewing insects. A good dormant spray used early in the year will be effective in eliminating many insects by destroying their eggs and killing survivors hidden in the cracks of bark and other handy places. Vigilance and a good spraying program will help prevent invasions of pests during the months to come. Dormant spraying should be done before the buds on the trees start opening. All sprays are toxic to pollenizing insects and care should be taken that no area being worked over by the bees is covered with toxic materials.

Soil conditioners, superphosphate (0-20-0), fertilizers and a good root stimulant should be among your supplies. Be sure you have an ample quantity of plant starter on hand. It is a must in establishing new plants. Use it according to directions and your planting failures will be very few indeed. Of course, you will place all these supplies where they are out of reach of children and pets and where they will not freeze.

Don't forget to invest in two or three small sprayers and keep them in a safe place. Label them so you will know for what purpose you use them. Nail polish makes a good marker for these items.

EARLY PREPARATIONS IMPROVE THE GARDEN

New Year's Day is the time for resolutions to be made, so they can be broken during the rest of the year. Of course we promise ourselves that this year is going to be different.

Let's resolve this year to make our gardens happier and more beautiful. Many things can be done early in the year so it will be easier to keep up with later developments at a time when our vigor and interest start to wane:

TREES. Many people think a good severe pruning every five years or so will do the trick. Not so. So much surplus wood will have to be removed that the tree may suffer from the pruning. Branches that should have been removed when young will leave gaping wounds when they are removed later. And the water sprouts will have produced a jungle of small branches that has turned the trees into thickets. It's so much wiser to have pruning done on a yearly basis so branches can be guided in their growth, surplus removed before it exacts a heavy toll from the tree, and diseases have made too much headway.

Arrange to have spraying done at the proper times. If a number of spraying jobs at certain intervals are recommended, follow that advice. A time schedule for pruning trees and shrubs can be found in literature available from the Extension Service. Beware the pruner who wants to prune everything in sight right now. He has much to learn and you have much to lose.

WEEDS. Some must be attacked before they put in an appearance. Crabgrass is one of the most noisome. It will become a thing of the past if Dacthal is applied to the lawns at the time the forsythias begin to show color. That means that all your leaves and other debris should be removed before that time. Dacthal should not be disturbed once it has been applied to the soil.

NEW BEDS. Lay out your plans, get materials ready and get the beds done as soon as possible. New beds should rest for a while and let the soil settle before taking on their new tasks.

CLEANING UP. Is there a tree, a shrub or other planting that has had its day? Remove it before the next growing season starts. Is there something superfluous in your garden that may do well for someone else? Find a new home for it before the planting season begins.

ADDITIONS. Are you planning to get new rosebushes, shrubs, vines or other permanent plantings? Study their requirements as to location and type of soil. Dig holes for them as soon as possible. Get the right type of soil for each ready for planting day. Set it beside the working areas so the new plants can be set in their places quickly. Let me tell you something from experience. If preparations have not been made for new plantings, the items ordered always arrive on a cold, blustery day when it is almost impossible to work outside.

TOOLS. If you don't always pick up your tools when you are through with them, paint the handles with a bright color so they will show up among the greens in the yard. Don't use an aerosol paint as it does not last, but get a good grade of paint that will withstand the weather. Allow a few days for tools to dry. If you are an optimist, do the job in an out-of-the-way place outside. If you know our spring weather only too well, look for a sheltered spot for the job. Apply two coats of paint if you have the time and you may be able to skip the painting job next spring. Be sure to wear your gardening gloves when you work with tools that have painted handles. They may cause your hands to blister otherwise. Or, you may wish to paint only the top six inches or so of a long handle.

MARKING PLANTS. Spring bulbs will soon fade and not too much later their foliage will dry and disappear. It's so easy to forget what plants were where, what colors they were and which ones needed moving or thinning out. Perhaps you might buy a package or two of the assorted colored plastic knife, spoon and fork sets. Then make up a code for your own use,

and mark the plant groups accordingly by driving the implements deep into the ground handle
first where they are not apt to be seen under the
protecting foliage. I use spoons to indicate the
blooms which have a cup and saucer - daffodils,
narcissus and so forth. The yellow spoons are
for the yellow blooms, white with a dab of yellow
acrylic paint for the white and yellows, pure
white for the white blooms, yellow with an orange
spot for blooms of that color, and so forth. The
forks are used for the tulips and acrylic paints
smeared on the tines to designate the color. The
knives are for the hyacinths and other bulbs.
These are then placed at each end of the group
that is to be removed and driven down deeply so
they are not apt to be seen by bright-eyed raid-
ers. Only the bulbs that must be thinned out,
removed, or protected during dormancy are marked.
        New spots for planting bulbs later in the
season are marked by short bamboo stakes driven
deep into the earth in a line indicating the areas
to be dug up. This is done before the foliage of
bulbs in the neighborhood disappears so one will
know where the empty spots lie.
        Don't you hate to remove a blooming iris
even though you no longer want it? Or perhaps
they are overcrowded and you do want to divide
them later. Yet, when they are gone the color or
variety is forgotten in a few days and you don't
remember which ones were to be moved. A little
device that has solved the problem for me has
been the paper punch. Again, I devise a code
to help me get ready for this mid-summer task.
On a plant which I wish to eliminate entirely, I
pepper one of the leaves with holes at random.
Or I may move it out immediately to eliminate later
work. On other plants I use a certain code - e.g.,
three dots in a horizontal row denote a pink self,
three dots in a triangle stand for a pink bi-color,
four dots in a row stand for a blue self, four
dots in a square formation stand for a blue bi-
color and so on. Write your code on a sheet of

heavy paper or cardboard and tape it inside your workshop door, the garage door, or wherever you know it will be safe until you need it. A code which shows up between the pages of a magazine in late October isn't going to be much help with the division of plants which took place in August. (Guess how I know!)

PROTECTING NEW PLANTS. We all know people who are so happy to accept plants offered, but will not take time to mark the places where they have been planted. Consequently they lose a great many that could have done much toward beautifying their premises. Newly set out plants need careful watering and extra attention until they have become established. Small plants hiding among others should be marked to be sure they are not neglected. Bamboo stakes with their tips dipped in a brightly colored paint will draw your attention to them until they can get along on their own.

Too often we hear this sad story - "My dog stepped right on the plant and ruined it." Or the culprit may be a child or a spouse who was helping with the work. If you are really in earnest about protecting new plants, invest in a bundle or two of bamboo stakes (I grow my own) for this purpose. Use them in lengths to accommodate the height of the plant until it is out of danger. After the plant has been safely set in the ground, place three stakes around it driving them into the ground at an angle. Bring the tops together like a teepee and tie them securely. You will find that it takes a very persistent dog or careless helper to damage all your newly set out plants.

STOPPING CUTWORMS. Just another little crime-stopper for our new gardeners. Sooner or later you will become acquainted with a fat little cutworm that loves tender young plants. You will detect his presence very soon. One fine day after you have proudly set out a number of tender

young plants, you will find that the little criminal
has been at work. Some of your plants will be
neatly severed at the base. Others that have not
been cut off completely will have begun to wither.
Digging close to the base of your plants, you may
find him. He is fat, grey, and curled up like a
doughnut.

Fortunately for us, his habit of living
and working in the top inch of soil is a help.
The best way to foil our little visitor is to place
a collar around the tender, young plant, pressing
it at least an inch into the soil and having it extend an inch or so above the soil line. The collars are easily made by using the sturdy half-
gallon milk cartons which will last until the plant
has developed a stem that is tough enough to withstand the onslaught of the little forager. Each
milk carton is enough for three collars. They are
placed around the plant and left for a month or
so until the stems have become thick and tough.

I start a great many plants in milk cartons. When it comes time to plant them outdoors,
I simply remove the bottom of the carton and set
the rest into the soil. Ready made protection!
Please don't do like the dear lady who buried the
collar completely because she didn't like the looks
of it. She was quite distressed that the cutworm
did not find it a barrier and severed her plants.

At one time, I had some banty chickens.
They kept the premises clear of cut-worms and
many other pests. They do little damage to
plants, and if you have a place where you can
keep them, they do wonders in keeping down the
pest population, and are especially fond of cut-
worms.

While there are other things that should
be done, these are among the chores most often
postponed until too late in the season, Believe
it or not, there seems to be no "tomorrow" for
earnest gardeners.

A NEW YARD OF YOUR OWN

So you are going to move into a brand
new home in a matter of weeks. It's a wonderful
feeling - a combination of happiness, excitement,
and even a generous amount of apprehension as
you review one of the greatest undertakings of
your life. Everything is so new and really yours
to mold as you wish.

Newest of all is the yard - so new it isn't
even levelled off yet. This is the part of your
new possession which is going to take most of
your planning because it is going to be the setting
for your new home. It will be the first impression
your visitors will have and it must represent your
personality and individuality.

A new yard presents many pitfalls, especially for one who has not done much gardening
in the past. Foremost among these is the fact
that most new home owners do not know how much
planting can be done in a given area. You've all
heard the old saying about the eyes being larger
than the stomach. Along the same line one can
say that the proposed landscaping is bigger than
the yard for which it is intended.

Other points to be considered are the
position of the house, the directions in which the
sun rises and sets, the patterns of the winds,
and the locations of the neighboring homes. If
another house is very close to yours, especially
if it is a rather tall structure, the shadow cast
by it will shade areas of your yard in varying
degrees. Sometimes a narrow space between two
houses becomes a wind tunnel creating an area too
cold for certain plants you would like to place
there.

Is your neighbor's yard higher or lower
than yours? Does one of them slope so drainage
will create a problem for the other? If you see
that a problem exists, why not get together with
the neighbor and rectify it before either of you
spend much money in landscaping. Your plants,

your neighbor and you will all be happier for having done this as soon as possible.

Next comes the fencing. A board fence can be both a blessing and a hindrance. It is a wonderful barrier against the wind and some plants will appreciate the shade that it affords during the hot part of the day. On the other hand its location may keep the sun from plants that need it in order to do well. Too, it is a snow and debris catcher. I just hope that you are on the right side of the fence where this is concerned. However, careful planning should make this a minor problem.

Soil conditions are of paramount importance. It would be wonderful if all you needed to do were to decide that the juniper bushes go here, the flowering trees there, and the rosebushes over there. The rhododendrons and azaleas will be in the bed on the east side, and the wisteria vine would climb up to shade the patio, and so forth. But a very important task must precede all these plans for planting. Those huge trucks that went back and forth with their loads of building materials have pounded the earth until it is as hard as cement. Then the bulldozer came in and buried all types of rubble as it massed heaps of earth only to level them again and tread them with its heavy feet. All this has compacted the earth so that the few inches of top soil scattered over the lot are all that the roots can invade with ease.

It all sounds frightening, doesn't it? It seems an insurmountable task, but taken a little at a time, you can have everything ready for next planting season. Lawn will do well in four to six inches of top soil providing there is good drainage underneath. If you will take the time to spade a generous amount of peat moss or a heavier soil conditioner into the lawn area and then smooth the earth, you can then sit back and wait until spring lawn planting time.

The flower and shrub areas will need

deeper soil. It should be spaded deeply with
humus incorporated. As much of the buried building debris as possible should be removed. Piling
the top layers of dirt to one side will make it
easier to dig deeper to loosen the soil. Into these
deeply spaded areas, place generous amounts of
humus of various sorts - peat moss, composted
material, steer manure which is not as hot as
horse manure and lasts longer, even lawn clippings.
Work it freely into the soil in place of the rubble
which you have removed. In February scatter a
few handsful of a high nitrogen fertilizer over the
area, and water it in well. This will speed up
the decomposing of plant matter as the sun warms
the earth during the approaching spring weather.
(I seem to hear some of the husbands to whom the
spading task falls expressing their opinions of the
work that lies ahead.)

After the soil has been replaced, you may
put your spade away for a while and concentrate
on garden magazines and flower catalogs. Look
at the pictures, read the descriptions carefully,
and plan your landscaping with care. Most people
have a tendency to overplant. Make sure that
the shrubs and trees you select are hardy in our
area. Also make sure that the size of your plants
will not be out of place in your yard. For
example, if your area is limited, don't decide on
Pfitzer junipers. Have you ever seen one that is
five or six years old that has not been pruned?
Plan for low growing shrubs under windows.
Place trees where they will not obstruct the view.
Trees can be used for privacy screens or to hide
an eyesore. Plant vines and climbers with a
purpose in mind.

Try to visualize the vast underground
network of roots that will be in your yard in a
few years. Each of these will take up its share
of food and water. That of course depletes the
soil. So why plant something that must be removed
later because it is proving to be a burden rather
than an improvement?

Here are a few points for you to keep in mind when deciding on your trees and shrubs.

- Determine whether it will be able to live in our area.
- Ascertain the size of your tree or shrub at maturity.
- Select a location that is suitable for the growing patterns of the tree or shrub.
- Choose a tree or shrub that will accomplish its intended purpose in a reasonable time.
- Remember that you should not place any permanent planting too near a building or fence and leave ample space for it so it will not become an obstacle.
- Be sure that the trees or shrubs are located for easy watering.

2. INDOOR GARDENING

Houseplants have a way of telling one that spring is coming. New leaves along the stems and branches, new shoots clustering on the stems and buds here and there are signs that the plant is getting ready for another season. In some cases, all that is necessary is more frequent watering and an application of fertilizer according to the specifications on the container.

But let's take a closer look. Notice the dead leaves, straggly stems and overcrowded pots that call for larger quarters for their contents. Also, is a good root-pruning balanced by the removal of top growth called for?

Another area that needs close attention is the soil condition in plant pots. Smell it. Many times a sour or other foul odor will tell you that it is time for a soil change. Prepare as much soil mix as necessary for the type of plant that needs attention. Before the day of the operation, water the plant well so it will be turgid and better able to stand the process. I always use a vitamin B-1 solution for watering.

Go about this task carefully, changing the soil, but disturbing the roots as little as possible. Be sure to use a clean pot for the plant's new home. Pots can be cleaned easily by scraping out old soil and incrustations, and soaking them in a chlorine solution. Some plants need only to have soil replenished. Refill the pots to their original level, eliminating all depressions. In many cases, this will "make do" for another year.

Don't get carried away at this repotting task. When the initial work is done, let the plants rest for a while. Don't fertilize until there is evidence of new growth which will indicate that the roots have adjusted to the new situation. To fertilize before this takes place may cause plants to die as the roots will not be able to cope with the concentration of fertilizer in the water.

It is time now to move your plants to the places that are most to their liking. Flowering plants should be where there is a good deal of light. Foliage plants do not need as much light.

To maintain a well-rounded specimen, plants need periodic turning. Some will need turning quite often, while others may be left for a week before they are turned a quarter circle at a time to keep them symmetrical. Fertilize according to directions, and do not let them want for water. Watch for insect pests and get rid of them immediately if any appear.

If you have a plant that does not respond to the directions in your various gardening books, try something different. It may be the answer. I had a five year old hoya which had grown well, but never bloomed. Many articles that told me how to make it happy were of no help. Then one summer, a friend gave me a gorgeous plant – really two hoyas in one pot. It was loaded with little panicles that indicated abundant blooms during the time that she had it in her home. It had been in a south window where it received a great deal of sun. Moreover, it was repotted three times in ten years. Following this example, mine was moved to a sunny window where it receives the sun's rays for a time each morning. The new hoya in the other south window is in a similar situation. Both plants are in a temperature range close to seventy degrees, or perhaps a little warmer when the furnace is running. The curtains are lowered at night to keep the chill from the windows away from the plants. I don't know if mine received inspiration from the other, whether it was embarrassed at its past bad performance, or whether the change in location and amount of light did it, but soon I found the start of some buds on it.

As a direct contrast to this incident, I

can cite another hoya of my acquaintance. This
one was root-bound in a container no larger than
an oversized coffee cup. It had two long strands
which had been trained along the wall in a rather
dark north room. In my opinion it received too
little light from a small window and a pane of
glass in the door. Yet it bloomed with clusters
of blossoms trailing over the wall.

If you have some house plants which,
given ample time, have not done as well as they
should, try a different location. However, you
must watch them carefully. Too much sun may
burn the leaves; it may be where a warm current
of air causes the edges of the leaves to brown, or
a draft may bother it. If any one of these things
is true, attempt to remedy the situation before
any harm is done. But do give something a try.

Now for fuchsias. It's time to prune them
now as they are waking up. Tiny, new leaves on
the branches indicate that they are getting ready
for a new season. Fuchsias bloom on new wood
and should be cut back severely so as to encourage new growth. A source from which I bought
most of mine advises that if we become frightened
at what we have done in pruning, we've done it
right.

Fuchsia pruning time is also time for
replacing the old soil, something that should be
done every two or three years. As usual, plants
should have been watered the day before this
takes place. Lift the plants out carefully, using
a trowel or other tool so as to disturb the root
ball as little as possible. Shake the plants so as
to dislodge some of the old soil, but not too much.
Then repot in a soil mix recommended for fuchsias
and water with a solution of vitamin B-1.

Return the plants to their winter home
since they won't be ready to go outside until
early June.

AFRICAN VIOLETS ARE PERFECT PLANTS FOR PEOPLE ON THE GO

African violets are one of the most adaptable of indoor plants. They like the type of environment which is also most suitable for us – temperatures ranging from 65 to 80 degrees with the cooler temperatures during the nighttime hours. A few degrees above or below that will cause them to feel uncomfortable and not able to function at their best.

They are the ideal plant for the working person who has no time during the day to tend to an outdoor garden, and for the apartment dweller or those who live in a condo and have no room for outdoor gardening. Best of all, they are the perfect hobby for the would-be gardener who because of some infirmity cannot get down on hands and knees to dig in the soil. One needs only to devote some time during the evening or in the morning to their welfare.

A common belief among those not informed is that African violets are only purple and shades thereof. Not so. They come in white, white with edges picoteed in various colors, pink – from very delicate shades to deep rose, fuchsia and magenta tones and blues as well as purples. Many come with white borders on the petals, crinkled petals and with variegated leaves.

For the best results, and for those who have no adequate source of natural light, African violets can be grown under artificial light. However, a south window or one so located that the plants receive a minimum of 10 to 12 hours of strong light each day is very satisfactory. I have grown mine in such a location for years.

They are sensitive to cold or a draft. When placed too close to a window, the temperature changes affect them. However, a distance of about three feet from a window where direct rays of the sun do not shine on them is ideal.

African violets are best watered from underneath - that is water poured into a saucer in which the potted plant sits. Watering a few this way is not much to ask, but when one has dozens, the easy way is to place the pots in a tray and pour water into it. A few trials should make one able to judge just how much water will saturate the soil and yet leave no extra water in the tray. Too, the water for these plants should be warm - really a few degrees above tepid.

African violets lend themselves well to propagation from cuttings of stems and leaves. One may find it interesting to try producing plants with this method.

African violets, like many other potted plants, are gross feeders. They thrive on a 12-36-14 formula and most African violet food is this. They may be fed at quarter strength each time they are watered, or full strength about every two weeks. The soil should be damp at the time of feeding. This is to insure that the plant is turgid and that the roots will not be damaged by the concentration of chemicals.

3. ROSES

Each year gardeners who have not grown roses before, decide on planting a rose garden. Planned and planted correctly, it will be a source of great pleasure. Roses are hardy and once established can survive a great deal of punishment, but if one plans to grow roses, why not give them the best of care?

There are a few points that should be observed to give roses the best possible opportunity for success. Roses need at least six hours of sun each day, so make sure that the proposed location does get at least that much. They want good drainage and deep soil so their roots can go down deep into the earth. Roses cannot compete with roots of other large plants in their beds, so don't plan to set them too near trees or shrubs that may share space with them. Roses need free air circulation both through each bush and through the bed as well. This prevents, or at least lessens, mildew and other fungal diseases.

Now, with all these things in mind, let's see about a rose bed. Does the spot selected meet all the requirements? Well and good! On the other hand, was the soil too compacted and did the spot tested not drain well? Is the soil thin, clayey, rocky? If so it should be dug up and replaced with good soil.

That's a lot of work and there is an easier way. Raised beds can be made in which to plant the roses. They are easier to weed and to give general care. The Washoe County Extension Service can supply good literature to help plan a raised rose bed.

Let's suppose that your rose bed, either one on ground-level or a raised bed, is ready for the rosebush. Personally, I stick to bare-root

roses for several reasons, the first being that I
find them more adaptable than packaged roses.
Next, I do not set out new plants until mid-April,
which is the time I ask nurseries to send me the
roses I ordered earlier in the year.

Dig a hole about a foot and a half each
way - across and to that depth. Place a handful
of superphosphate (0-20-0) in the hole and mix
it well with the soil at the bottom. Then spread
a thin layer of soil on top of that and build a
cone in the center of the hole. Be sure the cone
is high enough so when the rose is set upon the
cone, the bud union will be at the surface of the
bed.

Set the rose bush firmly upon the cone
so there will be no air pockets beneath it. Air
pockets are great plant killers. Spread the roots
out around the cone and fill the hole with soil to
which a handful of perlite and some compost has
been added. Water it well making sure all the
new soil is soaked.

The holes should also have been filled
with water and allowed to drain the day before
the plantings. This is done to make sure that
the surrounding soil is saturated and will not draw
water from around the root area.

Next, with a sharp pair of pruning shears,
cut down just above the second or third bud on
each cane. Cover the cut area with a generous
dab of white glue to prevent the rose borer from
attacking the cane and damaging it. Mulch the
canes with soil or finely ground bark.

As leaves sprout from the top buds,
remove a little of the soil to expose them. As
new buds show beneath the mulch, keep on doing
this by degrees until by early June all the mulch
has been removed, and the bud union itself is
exposed. Although established roses should be
fertilized, the first time about the time one prunes
them (in mid-April), new bushes should not be
fertilized until they are well established. In fact,
it won't hurt if they are not fertilized at all

Let's plant a rosebush.

discard

sub-soil

new soil

soil cone

Hole should be filled with water and allowed to drain.

Build cone of new soil with ½ cup of 0-20-0 mixed into it.

bud union

new soil

Set rosebush with roots around sides of cone. Be sure there are no air pockets and bud union is above soil level.

roots spread over soil cone.

Fill hole with top soil and water deeply.

Cut canes to 5 or 6 inches. Seal cut ends with white glue.

Mound extra soil or fine bark over top of canes for protection.

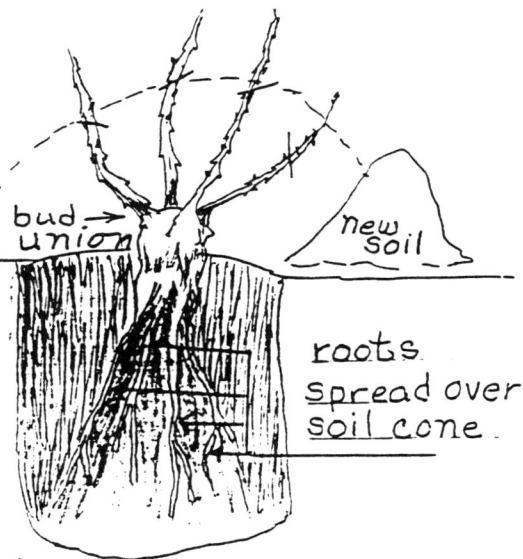

during their first year.

ROSEBUSHES NEED ATTENTION AFTER BLOOM CYCLES

By late June the first burst of bloom on our rosebushes is past its peak. Most roses have dropped their petals and those that are left are faded, sunburned and otherwise no longer at their best. The rosebushes themselves have put on a great deal of growth since the April pruning, and many of the bushes have centers so full of leaves and new growth that air cannot circulate freely through them.

At this time roses should be "dead-headed", that is, the spent and faded blooms should be removed. There is a right way to do this, but unfortunately, many do not know how it should be done. A cut on a rosebush, whether to pick a fresh bloom, or to remove growth, or to dead-head should always be done above a five-leaflet leaf. Deep in the axil of a five-leaflet leaf there is the start of another rose. A cut made indiscriminately anywhere else on the cane will promote the start of dieback, thus injuring a good part of the cane, and often preventing a new rose from appearing.

Whenever a cut is made on a rosebush, no matter what the reason, the cut should be sealed. Rose cane borers are active at this time and the tender pith is just the place the borer is looking for to lay her eggs. A generous dab of white or carpenter's glue will seal the opening, thus preventing damage to the cane.

A common practice to be discouraged for the sake of appearance is the cutting off of all spent blooms at the same level. This creates a flat-topped look to the bush when the next blooms appear. It looks much better if, whenever possible, the heights of the canes at which the spent blooms are severed are somewhat staggered.

At the time of dead-heading, another

necessary task should be done. Look down into
the center of the bush. If foliage there is so lush
one cannot see the canes themselves, passage of
air through the center of the bush will be impeded.
Careful removal of crossed canes, over-abundant
woody growth and the thicket of leaves is in order.
Another thing to look for are blind shoots. These
are clusters of leaves that look as if there should
be a bud coming up through the center - but
there will be no bud and no sign that there ever
will be one. Many of these blind shoots are small
enough to be removed by thumbpruning, but the
shears will do much better on the larger ones.
One should not cut above a blind shoot in dead-
heading. Nothing will ever bloom there and the
cane would suffer some die-back. Instead, cut
down to the first five-leaflet leaf. Of course, the
glue bottle should always be in evidence during
this task also.

Last, but not least, remove clusters of
leaves around the bases of the rosebushes. Bud
unions should be exposed to the light and air
should circulate freely around them. This will
also take care of removing a safe haven for some
pests that take advantage of shady spots.

Careful inspection for mildew and thrips
(those tiny living specks that quickly penetrate
to the heart of a rose) should be done now.
Spraying is in order - early in the morning before
the day becomes too warm - and of course, after
you have watered deeply the day before.

It's time now to think of the last feeding
with a complete rose food. Mid-July is the latest
time for this as later feedings will stimulate tender
growth which will be killed by one of our sudden,
early fall frosts.

ROSES NEED PREPARATION FOR WINTER

Late August brings about another phase
in the life of a rose. The fertilizers that have
been applied to stimulate growth and blooms are

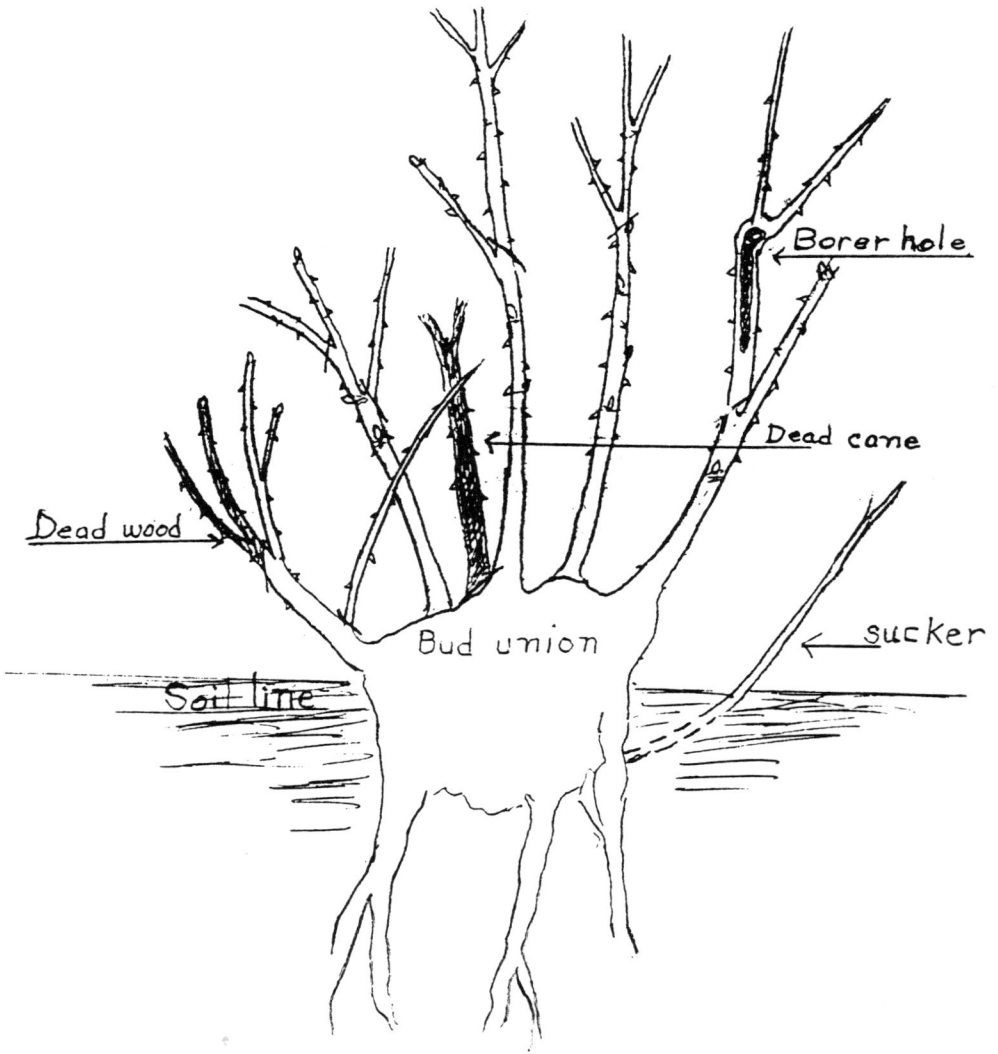

Borer hole

Dead cane

Dead wood

Bud union

sucker

Soil line

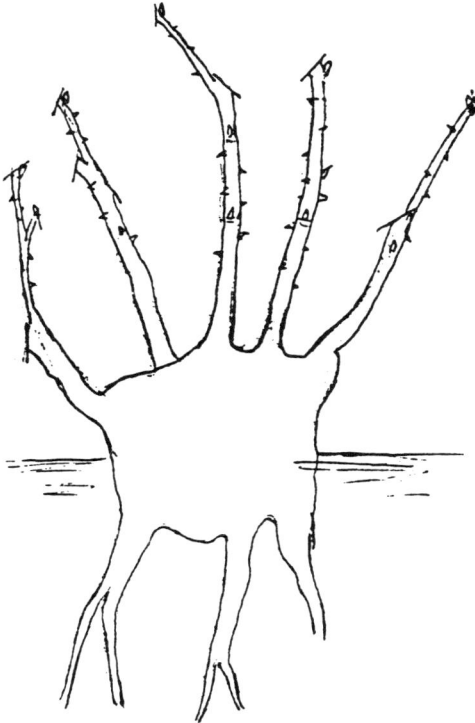

The two line drawings show the same rosebush
before and after pruning. Note that all dead
wood has been removed. The dead cane is gone
completely. The cane with the borer hole has
been cut off well below the damaged part. The
cane to the left has had the dead part removed -
sheared off at the point where a healthy part of
the cane remains. The thin cane that is growing
toward the center of the bush has been removed.

All cuts made by pruning should be sealed with
white glue or carpenter's glue. All cuts to
shorten or trim canes should be made on a slant
just above a bud.

now history.   Dead-heading after the first burst
of bloom has stimulated the production of buds
for the second showing of blooms which is now in
various stages.

Some roses are very prolific and dead-
heading was hardly over when they started blooming again.   Others are more inclined to take a
longer rest between blooming cycles and buds on
many of them are just beginning to open.

Normally, we have two blooming cycles
here, and occasionally after an unusually long
Indian summer, a third.   However, more often
than not, a really showy third burst of bloom is
interrupted by a cold spell that chills the buds
so that many of them do not open.

At this time of the year we must prepare
our rosebushes for the coming winter.   This is
done primarily by cutting down on the watering
program.   Watering should be done as usual –
deeply so that the entire root system is soaked.
But now we don't water as often.   Allow two or
three extra days between waterings.   Then grad-
ually add another day or so to the period before
the next watering.   Keep this up through the fall
until winter comes and regular watering is no
longer necessary.

Although no complete rose food should be
applied after mid-July, it is a good idea to give
roses a feeding of superphosphate (0-20-0) at this
time.   Spread the granules around the base of
each rosebush according to directions and scratch
them into the soil, being careful not to injure the
roots.   Water well after the application.   Superphosphate moves very slowly through the soil and
it will take a while before the rosebushes feel its
effect.   It gives the plants a stronger root system
and helps in the production of blooms, but will
not stimulate growth at this time when rosebushes
should be preparing for dormancy.

However, do not neglect watering, not
only the roses, but the rest of the garden if the
winter proves to be a dry one.   On a sunny day,

turn on the water and give everything a good
soaking. Be sure the deepest roots receive an
ample supply. Use an antidissecant on evergreens
- both those with needles and the broad-leafed
types. This will slow down the loss of moisture
during dry spells and because of the drying
winter winds.

4. GARDEN SENTRIES

Forsythia and bridal wreath immediately come to mind when flowering shrubs are mentioned. These springtime standbys are known to us all, but few of us stop to think of the many other shrubs that can brighten our gardens from February until fall.

Let's take a walk around and see what shrubs will do this. The evergreen daphne blooms in late February and early March in a protected place on the southeast side of the house. The fragrance is delightful and the breezes carry it to the nearby areas.

Forsythia blooms next, followed closely by bridal wreath and lilacs. Oregon grape follows with its glossy evergreen leaves and dense clusters of yellow blooms. This accommodating shrub will grow where there is only a half day of sun.

No prettier sight can be imagined than a Rose Tree of China in full bloom. The pink flowers are somewhat larger but resemble those of the flowering almond in shape and their manner of covering the leafless branches in early spring. The tree grows only four to five feet in height. I had one by the pool where its branches were reflected in the water at one side. I pruned the lower branches to encourage the top to spread out. It had a very pleasing form and did well in the shade of the taller trees that leaf out after its period of bloom has passed. It has since gone to make room for other things.

The magnolias, soulangiana and star types, do well in our area. Their buds are set during the preceding season, and the leafless branches are covered in early spring with bright blossoms. They must be protected from the sharp spring breezes if you wish to enjoy their flowers, because if they are out in the open, damage will occur. Magnolia grandiflora, which is evergreen and must also be given protection, grows into a magnificent tree with huge white flowers that bloom in the spring among the glossy dark green leaves.

Flowering almonds come in white and pink. They may be allowed to grow as shrubs, with part of their branches thinned out each year after blooming as I have done with my pink one. The white one is in a flower bed and constant pruning has kept the trunk clean and forces the top to branch out. In early spring it appears as a huge cluster of white blanketed branches which slowly drop their petals as the leaves take over.

Weigela and beauty bush bloom next, in scarlet and deep pink. They have not grown too large for me, because they have been planted in rather poor, rocky soil. However, some others I have seen have grown very large and are kept in bounds by pruning.

There are several types of mock orange from which to choose - large shrubs and dwarf types with single and double flowers. Their fragrance is like that of orange blossoms and the white-covered branches contrast beautifully with evergreens or trees with dark foliage.

As the season progresses, Rose of Sharon, which grows into a tall shrub unless it is kept smaller by pruning, is covered with hibiscus-like blooms in white, pink, rose, or lavender tones. It blooms profusely and over a long period of time.

Another shrub that blooms in summer is commonly known as vitex. This plant enjoys a long winter's nap, but it quickly leafs out and soon lilac-like blooms appear through July and last until frost. This attractive plant will grow over ten feet unless pruned back. It does well in a shrub border or as a lawn specimen.

Potentilla contributes flowers the size of a nickel in a bright yellow or combinations of red and yellow to the summer scene. This neat, compact bush asks for little care other than watering.

A smaller shrub, but a very attractive one, is blue mist spirea. This small, woody plant must be cut back severely each spring. New branches shoot out and grow quickly to almost three feet in height. Tufts of feathery blue flowers crown it during summer and early fall, and bees visit it with great glee.

Sunshine, deep soil, and plenty of water, accompanied by good drainage, will bring excellent results with any of the shrubs mentioned here.

PLANT A TREE OR TWO

Nothing gives a yard such a homelike appearance as trees and shrubs. They create a feeling of permanency, quiet and contentment. Well selected trees will give the homeowner years of pleasure and enhance the appearance of the property as time goes on.

Shade trees are for shade. That sounds like something we might say to a child but many of us, unthinking of the future, make mistakes which we later regret in setting out shade trees.

In a nutshell, the most common errors are the following:

- Trees set too closely together
- Trees too large for available space
- Plantings too close to a building or fence
- Trees placed so that their shade is cast in the wrong area
- Trees not suited to our climate
- Trees whose growth habits are not suitable for our purposes

The reasons for avoiding the above errors are obvious. Removing an established tree is usually an unhappy event for many times the tree has sentimental ties attached to it. I have a huge mulberry tree which is a perfect shade tree for the lower lawn. In summer we sit in its shade,

picnic under its spreading branches and admire
its beauty and the fact that it is pest free. It
drops all its leaves within days so there is no
long clean-up job in the fall. I hate to give it up
since it was one that my father started for me,
but because of my lack of foresight the disadvan-
tages of its present location are beginning to out-
weigh the good points. Although it is in the
lower yard it is so tall that it blocks the view
from the picture window in the living room. It
shades a great area of the flower beds and the
annuals set out there do very poorly because of
the lack of sun. Had I had the foresight to plant
it in the northwest corner of the lot, it would
shade two of the bedroom windows in summer, and
its shade would cast a welcome shadow on the
house during the hot days.

Unless you have lived in your present
home over a summer season and remember the
direction of the summer's hot sun, remember that
the sun moves farther north during that season
and you must plan the location of your tree
accordingly.

Consider the shape of your tree at maturity. It is hard for an inexperienced gardener to
visualize that slender whip which he has just
brought home as a full grown tree spreading its
branches, and casting its shade whether dense or
dappled over a large area. The four basic shapes
of shade trees suitable to our area are: - rounded,
either with branches set closely together or of a
spreading habit; - umbrella, spreading and low-
crowned; - pyramidal, roughly resembling a triangle; and - columnar, which are not too good for
shade but will fit well into a narrow space that
could not accommodate one of the more spreading
types.

If you have a large yard, or a tall house,
the fruitless mulberry and sycamore which are
both fast growing will produce ample shade in a
very few years. However, these trees have a
large spread, and unless you have a large enough

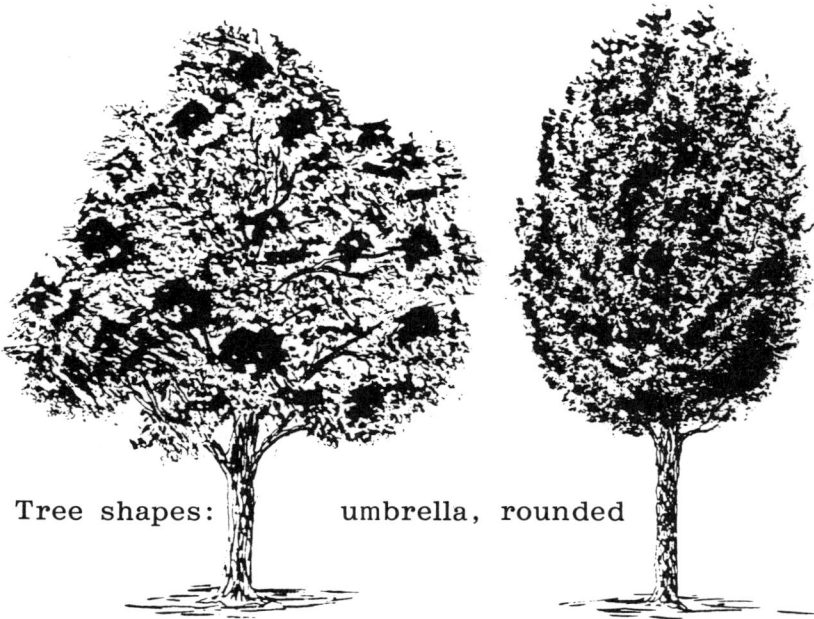

Tree shapes: umbrella, rounded

area, it is better to pass them by. The Hopa
crabapple, which becomes rather large and has a
spreading habit, is an attractive tree both for
its shade, and for the lovely blossoms that turn
into fine apples for jelly in the fall.
        Elms are outlawed in our area because of
a disease problem. The more reliable sources also
state that the so-called disease-resistant elms have
not been fully proven. Box elders grow fast and
are good-looking, but alas, box elder bugs and
fat little yellow and black caterpillars with white
bristles along their sides know it too. Willows
(also prohibited in our area) and sumacs do well
in wet places, but the former grows to a very
large size, and it is unwise to plant either where

their roots can penetrate a sewer system.

Among the suitable trees, most of the maples do well in our area. The sugar maple grows more slowly than the others that are obtainable locally. The mountain ash is an attractive and symmetrical tree that does well for us. Its clusters of berries are very much relished by the birds when they ripen. Catalpas are attractive trees with their huge heart-shaped leaves and cluster of blossoms in early summer. The seeds are produced in long pods that litter your lawn for a short time in the fall, or hang on the branches and clatter and rustle in the wind all winter. The Russian olive which has fine, grey-green leaves and wicked thorns casts a light, lacy shadow.

The birches are beautiful with their white bark and delicate foliage. They are better located where the winds do not blow on them too much. I know of only one birch in our region that seems totally happy. It is located with larger trees to the windward side, and planted in a lawn where it receives ample water. Birches are shallow-rooted (according to one source) and therefore water must be supplied in abundance.

The smaller locusts are fine trees for the home yard. They may be planted as lawn trees because their roots do not break the surface of the ground. However, if a black locust tempts you, I hope you have a large yard and can put it far from the house. They grow very tall, and their branches can snap easily in a windstorm.

Would you like something different? Horse chestnuts do well here although they grow slowly. Or perhaps you would like a pin oak for a specimen tree. Both have attractive foliage, the former produces clusters of blossoms early in the season, and the latter's leaves turn to bright fall colors at the close of the year.

Trees cannot do well without ample root space. If you have a yard built on hardpan, break up a large enough spot so you can give the

young tree a chance to establish itself. Fill in
the hole with good soil, be sure the drainage is
satisfactory, and plant according to directions.
Stake all young trees so they will not rock in the
wind. Be sure that they get ample water during
the first years until the roots go far enough down
to take advantage of sub-surface moisture.

Don't cringe when the nurseryman trims
a bare-root tree for you. He knows what he is
doing, and he knows that new gardeners are
afraid to do this initial pruning which gives new
trees a good start.

Some trees will grow rapidly and in a few
years will tower over their surroundings. Others
require many years to attain their ultimate heights.
Just relax and enjoy them for the pleasure they
give you as they grace your surroundings.

Tree shapes: pyramidal, columnar

5. COVERING IT UP

All of a sudden, when questioned, I couldn't think of some little plants - ground covers, border plants, rock garden plants, and so forth. It took only a little stroll through the back yard to remedy that. Many of these small plants have flowers, some of them insignificant, but in most cases very attractive ones. Too, with a variety of these plants, one can have blooms here or there all summer long.

Creeping phlox is perhaps the most showy of the creepers. Very early in spring, mats of white, lavender, pink, dark pink and cerise spread over the rose beds and creep over rocks. They remain in bloom for several weeks, and the mats of leaves increase in size if left undisturbed. When they are quite large, some soil placed on the branches and kept moist will encourage new roots to form. The stems can then be cut free in late summer and transplanted, their own new roots now taking care of them. Or, if you are a neat gardener, you may give your phlox an early shearing, and in August, pull out some of the shoots and plant them deep in the earth, where they will soon root.

Ajuga has dark leaves with a bluish-bronze cast. The small spikes of blue flowers are no more than six inches tall. This plant is neat and does not spread too quickly. It can be left undisturbed for a long time and makes a nice border as well as an interesting accent among rocks.

Aubrieta is a small plant with soft, fuzzy leaves. In early spring, a well-established plant blooms with dozens and dozens of pretty white or rosy lilac flowers. This plant should be cut back after blooming, as it becomes untidy otherwise, and will eventually dwindle away. Several clumps of these plants tucked in corners, under shrubs, and close to rocks will bloom at the same time as the white-flowered rockcress, and the two will make an attractive picture. Rockcress, too, needs a severe haircut after blooming, but will continue growing until frost.

Snow-in-summer blooms a little later. Its grey-leafed mat stands a foot high and the five-petaled white flowers are the size as a dime. It makes a fine ground cover for the area where lilies are planted, because their roots must be kept cool. The same is true of clematis, which will welcome a carpet of this creeper to cool its feet.

Myrtle and bishop's weed, both of which are very invasive and grow profusely, are good plants for a shady area. Bishop's weed disappears during the winter, but myrtle is evergreen. Both can be kept in check by pulling out the excess plants the day after they have been watered. Many of the roots come out with them, so it isn't too hard to do. Their ability to grow in a practically sunless spot makes them useful to many gardeners.

The sedums are many, and their succulent leaves are of many shapes, sizes, and variations of color. The masses of small blooms range from near-white, through the pinks, and round out their gamut of colors with deep red tones. They bloom far into the year, when most other creepers have retired from the color parade for the season. Some make excellent dried arrangements.

The plants mentioned so far are perennials and will be with me for a long time. Cuttings have increased the phlox and many are cut back severely to be kept within bounds. In the spring, when the smaller plants have a few blooms to show their color, they can be successfully moved by taking a clump of earth with them. Early tulips pushing their noses through clumps of creepers are beautiful.

Ajuga produces small plants that can be

lifted carefully and moved elsewhere. Snow-in-summer and rockcress can be increased in the same manner as creeping phlox. Two popular annuals for the border are ageratums, which grow in small mounds covered with tiny tufted flowers in blue and white, and the dark blue lobelia. Both are good bloomers, neat and compact in appearance, and attractive all summer long.

St. John's wort is very invasive and hard to eradicate. It serves well to cover a steep slope and to prevent soil erosion.

Lamb's ears with grey leaves that feel like lambs' ears, has spikes of purple flowers in early summer. Though it spreads easily, it can be controlled with little effort.

DO FENCE ME IN

"Do Fence Me In" should be the theme song of many interesting plants which find their way into our gardens. Perennial plants that have a tendency to take over are of many types – climbers, creepers, uprights – tall and short, ground covers, and attractive floral specimens. All of these have invasive root systems. Some spread very rapidly, while the progress of others is much slower. The amount of water they receive, location, and fertility of the soil also contribute to the speed with which they spread.

Among these one finds the mint groups, Mexican primroses, false dragonhead, Chinese lanterns, berry vines, St. John's wort, silver lace vine and various creepers.

Mint, which likes a moist situation, increases very rapidly and should be cut back severely by tearing out the root system where it is not desired. I have a large clump by one of the water taps. It has spread profusely, and several times a year I remove large portions to keep it in bounds.

The Mexican primroses are planted with a stone wall to their backs and a resistant lawn in front of them. These and an occasional foray with the mowing machine keep a pink profusion confined.

Some Chinese lanterns are against a wall behind one of the rose beds, and another group is in a situation similar to that of the Mexican primroses. This helps to keep them under control.

The raspberry canes are planted in an area that also runs along a wall. The annual pruning at the end of the fruiting season helps hold them back, but when plants stray too far from their home base they are pulled out when the earth is damp. Large portions of the roots are readily torn out, and they are easily held in check if one does not put off the task until the area is completely over-run.

Lace vine, a beautiful, airy plant covered with panicles of lacy flowers, grows rapidly sky-ward, covering buildings and fences, and hiding unsightly spots. It offers shade, yet is not so dense as to discourage a breeze from blowing through. I planted one in a sunken redwood planter from which the bottom was removed. The surrounding area is so far uncultivated, but the roots have made no attempt no force their way out of the planter. Once or twice a year, I clip off shoots that are growing low on the plant and tear out top growth that is becoming too abundant. The plant covers the edge of the carport roof, keeps out the sun, and is attractive all summer long.

Three creepers are a boon for the problem shady area where nothing else will grow. One is the green and white bishop's weed that somewhat resembles a variegated ivy leaf and will grow to a foot in height if it receives ample water. The plant, which spreads rapidly by means of runners, dies down in winter and returns timidly in the early spring, acquiring courage as the earth becomes warmer. Myrtle, with its blue-purple blooms, and St. John's wort, whose dollar-sized bright yellow flowers sport a tuft of silky stamens, are both evergreen. They lose some of their gloss and take on a slightly weatherbeaten look in winter, and the blooms disappear during the cold weather, but the presence of green still gives a promise of warmer days.

The three creepers do not limit themselves to shade, but will send out runners and roots that invade neighboring areas. When they go beyond the bounds I wish them to observe, they are given a good soaking. On the following day, when the roots are more prone to release their hold on the damp earth, I pull them out. This may have to be done two or three times during a season, but their benefits are worth the time involved. They will cover a steep slope, a rocky area where it is difficult to raise more demanding plants, the other side of the driveway that receives the seepage from the neighbors' watering, or any other area that would otherwide be barren.

VINES - COLOR AND CAMOUFLAGE

When fall color is everywhere, it is a good time to look at vines. Unfamiliar ones may have caught your attention with their brilliant colors in a neighbor's yard, as you drive down the street, or during a day in the country. Vines cover a multitude of sins - old fences, unsightly spots, walls that need a softening effect, tall poles, pergolas, trellises and just about anything. I'm sure that public utilities will object to their poles being covered with a mass of greenery, but a vine growing to eye level or just above on one of these should cause them no hardship.

Vines can be grouped loosely into three categories - flowering, fruit-bearing, and decorative leaf types. Several vines can qualify under more than one of the headings mentioned. Some are evergreen, but most are deciduous, their bare limbs no longer hiding those spots which were so well covered during the summer months.

One of the most attractive and useful of

mine is the honeysuckle which blooms all summer long and bathes us in fragrance when we go through the carport and down the steps into the back yard. It is evergreen and in the winter affords some shelter and berries for the birds. Because of its location, it also parries much of the snow which would otherwise sift into the car port.

A huge silver lace vine which grew from a start that a friend gave me, shades the western side of the car port. In summer a cloud of tiny petals drop from it and cover the ground only to be blown away by the first breeze. Its small, intricate branches also serve to keep the snow out of the car port, and together with the honeysuckle cover most of the open parts.

The trumpet vine which another friend gave me did not do well when it was located on the west side of the house where it received little water. Later I moved it to a corner by the front fence where it was joined by a start of one from another yard. Because of the ample water and sunshine all day long, they both decided to show what they could do under the right conditions. Their long shoots were trained to climb the unsightly night-light pole. By the next season they had reached many feet above the ground, and bright orange trumpets appeared in summer to enhance the attractive leaves.

Virginia creeper, that lovely vine that is a blaze of red in the fall of the year, trails along the garden fence its branches loaded with small dark berries that are picked by the quail as the first snow flies. Another Virginia creeper climbs a trellis attached to the storage shed. This vine is prone to be victimized by red spider, so dousing with cold water and spraying with malathion or diazinon at the first sign of infestation is necessary. The lacy leaves and the blaze of fall color are well worth the effort. Be careful about where you plant this one as it takes over very readily.

After two attempts at starting a Boston ivy from a friend's lovely climber, I have succeeded in growing one that covers the outside of the brick wall which forms the jutting tower for the kitchen windows. The tower is completely covered and looks as if it might be part of the castle which hid the Sleeping Beauty for so long. Only the east window breaks the green expanse during the summer. The vine has now grown around the corner to the east, and turned the next corner to hang over the front door. An occasional stripping removes the parts of the vine that climb over the window screens or attach themselves where I do not wish them to go. Tiny birds find the berries edible and the vine and the nearby pyracantha offer winter shelter.

Clematis vines are beautiful, come in many colors, and bloom over a long period of time. Two white ones - Lanuginosa candida and Henryi are on the south side of the house, their roots shaded by myrtle and other low growing plants. The popular and hardy Nellie Moser, a lavender with rosy pink ribs on its petals grows by the Lanuginosa. A new one for me, a late-blooming yellow one is next to Nellie Moser. Since they bloom at different times, the colors do not clash, and the lacy leaves of the yellow one form an attractive network over the wall. Clematis vines like the sun, but their roots must be kept cool. They want good drainage, but must have ample water. After the petals have fallen, the dry centers of the blooms make attractive, fragile materials for dried arrangments.

If you have a place for them, what better vines can you plant than those of the grape? Many grow well in our area. Concords, Malaga and Thompson seedless produce for us every year. They like deep, rich soil, lots of water during the early part of the season, and sunshine all day long. They must be supplied with supports so they can climb into the light. Grapevines should have water curtailed somewhat toward the early

A section of grape arbor.

fall season so the grapes will be sweeter as the
sugar content rises when they ripen. Don't let
them suffer. They still must have enough water
to keep the vines and leaves turgid.

Grapevines are pruned in February. If
you want the vines to cover areas for shade, the
pruning should be light. If you want to force
the production of grapes, the pruning should be
very severe. Frequent sprayings are necessary
to ward off red spider and leaf hoppers. Keeping
the ripening fruit from the birds proves an interesting pastime. Nylon net secured on the stem
over a grape cluster and coming well below the
bottom of the grapes proves frustrating to the
would-be thieves. It is not necessary to under-
stand bird language to know what they are saying
as they survey the many nylon petticoats draped
over their favorite food.

All the vines mentioned in this chapter
are well suited to our climate. Since they are
strong growers with large root systems, they need
a deep bed of rich soil. They should have good
drainage and all of them should have at least half
a day of sunshine. Grapevines should have sun
all day to produce the best fruit. Cuttings from
most of these vines can be started in early spring.
Bare-root stock may be obtained then, also. If
you are lucky, you may be able to find a potted
specimen at a nursery.

Grape cuttings made at pruning time should
be from one to one and a half feet long. They
should be buried with at least two joints under
the soil and kept damp until growth starts. After
that water them whenever necessary. The following spring they may be moved to a permanent
place in the yard.

A wisteria vine in bloom is a beautiful
thing. Wisterias must have the tops of their
vines in the sun in order to be induced to bloom.
A southern exposure is good, and a bamboo cane
for support of the young plant will be welcome
indeed. My oldest wisteria has huge limbs twisted

44

around a bamboo cane which cannot be seen, but
the vigorous plant has used it for a climbing post
to reach the top of the sun deck and spread its
clusters of blooms all over it.

6. GLADS & DAHLIAS

It is time for some spring planting.
Several plants - gladioli, dahlias, geraniums and
chrysanthemums - can be dealt with in late April
and early May.

If you live in one of the warm microcli-
mates, you may be able to stagger three plantings
of gladioli, providing you get the first group
planted in April and the other two from ten days
to two weeks apart. If you live in a cooler area,
it may be wiser to plan only one planting, as one
of our usual September frosts will be sure to get
late bloomers.

Work your area for glads, dahlias and
cannas by adding compost, well-rotted steer
manure and perhaps a bit of perlite to the soil.
Add a generous sprinkling of superphosphate
(0-20-0) and work it in well. You should have
good drainage in areas where tubers and corms
are to be planted, or they may rot instead of
producing blooms.

Those of you who are familiar with my
yard may have seen the row of low-growing dahlias
at the south end of the front lawn. It was several
years before I hit upon these blooms to border
the edge of the lawn. I had tried petunias, but
no matter what color I chose, they clashed with
some of the roses in the border just below. Then
I tried asters with the same result.

Finally I decided upon Unwin dahlias, the
small plants that are grown from seed and appear
for sale in four-inch pots in the spring. There
are many advantages to these in a planting such
as mine. They are inexpensive and of reasonably
good size when they appear on the market. They
come in assorted colors and it is not until the
buds show color that one is aware of the many

different hues that one has planted.

If the spent blooms are removed, they will keep blooming all summer until a killing frost strikes them. There is another advantage. By fall they have developed a clump of tubers which, if stored carefully, can be planted again the following year. After the killing frost has turned the tops black, I let the plants sit for a week or so. Then I cut off the tops leaving about four inches of the stalk protruding above the earth. This is done to allow the tubers to mature somewhat before I dig them up about two weeks later.

In the past I have tried old sawdust, peat moss or a soil conditioner in which to store the tubers. However, I have found that the best medium for this purpose is good, clean sand. Too, I have some old tubs which I use to store the tubers.

The novice, upon digging up a dahlia clump and seeing ten or more robust tubers will be happy with the idea of dividing them among friends or planting a great bed of dahlias. It doesn't work that way. Only a tuber that has a part of the old stem attached will grow and bloom. The rest should be discarded as they will produce nothing.

Clumps, when dug, should not be divided; an entire clump should be stored. Each clump should be dusted with diazinon dust to kill any vermin that might be clinging to the soil. Do not shake or wash the soil off, but leave some on the tubers. Of course you will place your containers for winter storage in their winter homes before filling them with sand and tubers. A location with an even temperature (around forty degrees) is ideal. The root cellar, the space under a house (where the heat of the furnace will not affect the tubers) or any outside building where the temperature does not drop too close to freezing should do, providing the containers are large and the supply of sand ample.

I place a layer of sand - two inches or

so – in the container, then place a clump of tubers on it, put in more sand until the tubers are covered, add another clump and cover it. If the clumps are small, they may be placed close together. Three to five clumps of tubers can be placed in one container, and the process is repeated until all the tubers are covered. Be sure the clumps of tubers don't touch each other. The layer of sand covering the top should be at least three inches deep.

In early March I sprinkle a cupful or two of water on each container; I repeat the process in April. When May comes, after I have prepared the beds for the tubers, I take them out and check carefully to see which ones can be cut with a portion of the stalk attached. I'm not surprised if out of a cluster of nine or ten, I can get only two or three good ones. The salvaged ones will always be more than enough to plant next year. Young dahlias are very tender, so if when new growth shows, chilly weather threatens, an A-frame over the plants will keep them from freezing.

Plant cannas as you do dahlias. Prepare the soil and see to it that they are where they will get at least half a day of sunshine. Dahlias prefer a full day if possible.

Spring is the time to make cuttings from your chrysanthemum plants. The new shoots should be from three to five inches high. These may be started in damp perlite or in soil. The medium, whatever you may choose, should be damp and the plant, from which the cuttings are taken, turgid from a good watering the day before. With a sharp knife, cut off shoots that are about three to four inches long. Strip all but the top three or four leaves, dip the end of the cuttings in a rooting medium and insert gently into the soil. Place them in a sheltered situation until roots begin to form.

If you are one of those who tends your plants carefully each day, you may then plant them out in the garden, making sure to protect them from the elements until they are firmly established. Otherwise, it will be wiser to plant them in 4-inch pots until they are large enough to withstand the rigors of life in the flower border.

Geranium cuttings may also be made now from the straggly plants that were stored in the basement or in the greenhouse last winter. There is one very important difference in making geranium cuttings as opposed to cuttings from chrysanthemums. Geranium cuttings should be allowed to callous for several hours or more before being inserted into the starting medium. I used clean sand for this the last time I made cuttings from geraniums. Ten cuttings and they all became sturdy plants. I dipped the ends as usual in a rooting medium, inserted the cuttings in planting medium and put them in a sheltered area. When well rooted, I transferred them to pots which in time were put in larger pots with the space between them filled with fine bark. These were then placed on the sun deck where they spend the summer.

Many other plants can be divided now. Be sure that they have been well watered the day before and that the new place for them is ready. Use a sharp spade, cut down deeply so as to sever the part to be moved completely, and place at the same depth in the new spot. Water well with a solution of vitamin-B-1 and protect from the sun for several days until well established.

Many plants thrive after being divided thus, but several do much better if cuttings are made from them. Chrysanthemums are definitely in this group.

Foliage from our spring blooming bulbs will be pretty unsightly in a little while. Try not to see it, and leave it to produce food to feed the bulbs. Although it is recommended that bulbs be left alone during the dormant period into late summer you may have to move them earlier for some reason. Moving them to another home may be accomplished by lifting the whole bulb mass without disturbing the soil and placing the clump

in a box where you will leave it until planting
time in the fall. Do not overwater. As soon as
the foliage had died down, place the box in a cool
corner and leave it alone until planting time. Or
you may wish to move a clump to another spot
before you forget where the empty space is. Dig
a hole in the new location, lift up the entire soil
mass and bury it to its original depth. It will
never know that it was moved if you are careful
not to disturb the roots. Otherwise you may lose
the bulbs.

7. FOREVER YOURS

Last spring you were out in one of the local nurseries intent on buying new plants for your garden. You asked a clerk if a certain perennial would bloom this year, and you were told that in some cases you would not get flowers from it until next year. Then you asked about another and another, and upon receiving the same answer you left them and bought some annuals.

I wanted to tell you that perennials are the mainstay of your garden. Year after year these old friends come back to form a more luxuriant background for your colorful annuals that must be replaced every year.

Almost three hundred different types of perennials greet me as I work in my garden cleaning up the winter's debris and preparing the flower beds for the coming season. Remember that perennials are of many kinds - flowering trees, shrubs, bulbs, herbaceous plants that disappear completely during the winter and those that maintain little clumps of green all year to mark their places in the garden.

Perennials do not all bloom at once, nor does their period of bloom cover an entire season. The first snowdrops and violets brave the late winter days in February. These are followed by the early bulbs and then by a never-ending succession of bloom that changes every few weeks and closes with the late chrysanthemums which put on their show through the last days of Indian Summer.

Perennials once established need little care to keep them going for years. As the clumps grow larger you will have to divide them occasionally. This is a pleasant task because you can share and exchange with others. All perennials need not be divided each year, nor are all perennials to be divided at the same time of the year. A few examples are the composites which are divided as soon in the season as new growth is long enough for cuttings or clumps are sturdy enough to separate. Iris can be moved almost any time after blooming, so long as this is done early enough for them to establish new root systems. Oriental poppies are divided in late August and peonies are divided in September.

Perennials thrive on division – in fact some will eventually die without it. The composites which include the different large daisies, hardy asters (also known as Michaelmas daisies), and the many types of chrysanthemums should be divided every third or fourth year to keep them in vigorous condition. A single poker plant can become a dozen plants in four year's time. The various campanulas produce new plants each year as do day lilies, lily-of-the-valley, phlox, hostas, montebretias and many others. Lupine drops seeds that, although they produce plants not true in color to the mother plant, offer many lovely surprises.

Irises multiply rapidly and should be separated every three or four years. Peony plants which grow larger with each year may be left undisturbed indefinitely, or they may be divided in fall to form new plants. Oriental poppies grow more luxuriant with each year. In fact many of them produce fertile seeds that surprise us with flowers unlike their parents. Hibiscus clumps send out more stalks as they grow older and a succession of blooms lasts from late July into August. Delphiniums will bloom twice if you cut off the first stalks after they have bloomed and give the plant a good feeding. Daisies will bloom as long as you will take the time to keep the dead flowers removed.

Ground covers may seem expensive, but when you consider how much space can be covered by a flat of these plants, you will find that you are making a very good investment. In no

time carpets of creeping phlox, ajuga, snow-in-
summer or myrtle will cover problem areas.
Myrtle will grow in the shade.

Vines can hide many unsightly spots,
climbing over fences, rocks, posts and buildings.
They will cover walls and pergolas, trellises and
the lath-house that shades your fuchsias and
begonias.

Sedums, such as hens-and-chickens, are
ideal in rock gardens or in areas where watering
is a problem. Although they practically disappear
in winter, spring finds them ready to produce
huge clusters of little "chickens" and succulent
growth that is well able to stand drought and a
certain amount of neglect.

A growing season is really so little time
to wait. When you buy perennials and plant them
in your permanent border, the colorful annuals,
that will last through one season, give you tem-
porary beauty while the perennials are taking
hold and preparing to give you years of pleasure.

Get together with some friends and plan
to go back to the nurseries for some perennials.
Each of you can buy several different ones and
in no time at all you'll have extra plants to trade
with each other. Your new plants will flourish
and your flower beds and borders will bring color
to your garden all year long.

Experienced gardeners will offer you
plants if they feel that you are really in earnest
about growing things. Pick them up when they
are ready for moving and plant them according to
directions. You may not have a permanent place
located for them, but there is no reason why you
can't place them almost anywhere for a season
and, when you have selected their place, move
them.

Plan for a larger perennial bed now. It's
so much more satisfactory to say, "I'm gald I
did", than, "I wish I had".

PEONIES ARE FOREVER

No more beautiful perennial than the peony can gladden your garden in the bright, colorful months of May and June. Huge clumps of this gorgeous flower bloom with little attention after the initial planting. Few insects and diseases bother them and their foliage lasts into the fall. The graceful clumps of leaves turn yellow and red throughout the last days of the season and then are cut down during the pre-winter cleanup.

Because of their foliage, I plant peonies at the front of a border. They hide the unsightly leaves of the Oriental poppy as they die down, and the stiff leaves of the iris that stand behind them. I do not cut off the leaves of the iris, but leave them to manufacture food for the new rhizomes that are forming.

When I started gardening I had ten peony plants – all beautiful double specimens in white, pink suffused with white, rose, and a beautiful red. I bought several other attractive ones, and made new plants from divisions of old ones that had become unusually large in the rich new soil and the sunny hillside location. Then a friend gave me a start from her beautiful Mikado, a single, deep red Japanese peony with a spectacular center of huge golden stamens. This started me on the single varieties and I now have several lovely plants.

Some time ago, a young peach tree which grew from a pit dropped in the flower bed disputed a corner with one of the new singles. Unwilling to harm either, I left them together for two years, but one spring something had to be done. The young tree, now as high as the floor of the sundeck had to be moved, so the day after a good soaking this was done. We dug a place for it in the corner of the vegetable garden and lifted it carefully so as not to disturb the roots. Part of the peony plant came up with it, and we left it with the tree and planted it in the new

ation. The other part of the peony evidently
d not suffer from the unseasonal disturbance,
nd although it did not bloom that year, it survived and did bloom the next spring.

Besides the beautiful singles with their
interesting centers, and the gorgeous doubles that
are sometimes six inches across, there are the
strikingly attractive Chinese tree peonies. Unlike
the others, they do not disappear in winter for
they have a woody stem. They attain a height of
four feet at maturity and the woody part should
never be cut back. Because of their size and
nature of their growth, they should be planted in
a location where they are protected from the wind.
Evergreens, walls, tall fences and buildings are
excellent for this purpose. The new plants should
be mulched during their first winter with a light
material that will not pack. The mulch should be
applied after the ground has frozen.

Peonies like a sunny location, rich garden
soil and, of course, good drainage. I dig a deep
hole for each new plant, and as for all other
plants with heavy fleshy roots, I place superphosphate (0-20-0) in the bottom of the hole and mix
it well with the soil. Then I place a layer of
clean soil on top of that which was mixed with the
superphosphate. The peony is then placed at the
proper level and the hole is filled with soil. I
soak the area with water to which a root stimulant
has been added. As the years go on, the roots
of the peony will extend down and take advantage
of the fertilizer placed there for its use.

Peonies should be planted so the new bud
tips are covered with only one inch or so of soil.
They will not bloom if planted too deeply. The
plant needs the cold to make it bloom, so do not
worry about the little bud tips freezing. You will
find them peeping through the snow in late March
and they will then bloom happily in May. The
buds may suffer from a severe, late freeze in
April or May and not bloom, but fortunately this
doesn't happen very often. Strangely enough,

gardeners in the southern states cannot grow peonies successfully because their winters are too warm.

Because they do not go dormant until fall, I place peonies anywhere since their foliage is always attractive and they do not mind water even after their blooming period is over. They are in front of flower borders, between rosebushes, in special pockets in the plant terraces and in a ten foot bed in front of the greenhouse. They can be left undisturbed indefinitely and grow larger and more beautiful as the years go by.

Usually peonies will not bloom the first year after planting. However if they should send out a few buds, it is wise to remove them so the young plant will gather more strength during its first year in the ground. (I must confess that I always leave a bud or two. I'm just too curious to see what the new bloom looks like!)

Peony colors range from white through the pinks, rose tones, and finally, a deep red. Besides these standard colors, yellow, purple and lavender peonies are also available. I have not seen any of these and do not know how they would do in our area. They are also somewhat higher in price than the first ones mentioned.

Should a new plant send up very slender leaves instead of the broader ones, chances are you have planted it too deeply. You can either mark the spot and dig around the plant to remove part of the soil, or better yet, wait until fall and dig up the plant resetting it at the proper level.

Be sure to mulch during the first winter. My evergreens get a late pruning quite regularly because I use the tips of the branches for mulching new perennials to help them through the first winter in their new home.

Finally, peonies may be attacked by a virus disease known as botrytis. It can be prevented, but not eradicated. It can be detected easily because it causes the plant to become sickly and the leaves shrivel and wither and finally turn

black. When you notice this, pull out the plant
entirely. Either burn it or throw in into the
garbage can. Burn all affected leaves and spray
the earth around the plant base with phaltan. It
is also wise to use a phaltan spray in the spring
before any sign of disease is evident. All peony
leaves should be cut off and destroyed in the fall,
and the surrounding area cleared of summer's
debris. Phaltan sprayed on tulip beds will prevent botrytis in tulips, also.

THE TALL ONES

A very interesting group of plants that
range from short spikes no more than a foot tall
to strikingly beautiful six foot giants should give
you many ideas for landscaping your area. The
plants mentioned here produce their blooms on tall
spikes, or, less commonly, on spikes which develop
side branches and are known as racemes.

The delphinium is the most spectacular of
these. Since the various hybrids have been developed, it is one of the most attractive of the tall
plants. I have found the hybrids rather short-
lived for our area, and must replace a few every
two or three years, but their beauty and wide
range of colors makes them worthwhile. Plants in
four-inch pots are available at all nurseries, some
of them with a blooming stalk, others with the
flowers just forming. I buy the latter whenever
possible because when they do bloom, the flowers
will last longer. Perhaps, if you are lucky, the
plant will send up a second shoot the first year.
The second year, if you have selected a good
spot, staked the plant carefully, and fed and
tended it well, you should be rewarded with three
or four spikes, some of them reaching six feet in
height.

My favorites are the Round Table and
Astalot series. These range from pure white
Galahad, beautiful pink and orchid Guenevere,
Lancelot in white and sporting a black bee, King

Arthur in royal purple with a white bee, to the handsome Black Knight as deep a purple as King Authur, but with a black bee making it the darkest of the group. A bee in a delphinium is that small appendage growing in the center of each bloom.

Summer Skies, Blue Bird and Blue Jay, a series of blue delphiniums, light up the garden with their clear, true tones. They are not quite as large as the first ones mentioned, but are hardier. I have some eight year old plants in the garden that are still doing well.

Lupines, especially the Russell group, have an amazing range of color. Their attractive foliage is an eye-catcher even when they are not in bloom. Many are of one color and a great number of them have centers of contrasting hues. Like the delphinium, they will bloom again if the first spikes are removed after the blooms have faded. Several of these plants in the perennial bed make a striking picture. Small plants purchased now and planted among other flowers, will bloom next spring. The long season will give them plenty of time to become established. Mark them so you will be sure to keep them watered, and other plants will not cover them as the season progresses.

Lupines are very prone to be hosts for aphids. The clumps must be inspected often, and at the first appearance of the pests, malathion should be used. A strong, water spray does not help in this case because the leaves are so delicate, that a stream of water strong enough to wash off the pests, will damage the leaves. Make your malathion solution somewhat weaker than full strength, or the small inner leaves will be burned. After the sun goes down, splash the solution generously over the plant making sure you get all of it wet. Again, it is better to have your solution rather weak and repeat the application than to burn the plant.

Red hot pokers, formerly known as tritomas,

which originally came only in part red and part
yellow, now come in red-orange, orange, coral
and very pale yellow.   A clump of this plant becomes larger with each succeeding year and should
be divided in a few years.   Make your divisions
early in the spring or in September.   These
plants come in robust sizes, or in smaller, daintier
sizes suitable for various locations and purposes.

The foxglove we grow in this area is a
biennial (although a perennial form also exists).
From it, digitalis is manufactured.   Plants set out
in August or later will bloom the following year.
Most foxglove comes in white or pink tones.   Some
have a lavender cast.   These plants are perfectly
happy in the shade with only the filtered sunlight
coming through openings in the branches overhead.
They bloom very well in late June and early July
and then make way for other things that wait for
their places in the dappled shade.   (Foxgloves
are toxic and care should be taken so children
and pets won't be poisoned).

Have you ever seen a yucca with more
than five hundred blooms on one stalk?   Several
times, such beauties have been mine.   People
driving along the street have slowed down to get
a better look at this tall stalk with its cluster of
white bells.   A friend gave me a start of this
desert plant many years ago, and since then a
number of plants have been separated from the
original.   They are scattered here and there
among the flower beds.   Yucca does well outside
the fence where it gets watered only occasionally,
and it is equally happy by the pool where it gets
a great deal of water while other plants are being
soaked.   The tall stalk, as thick as a broom
handle, grows quickly to its full height.   Short
stems shoot out at right angles to the main stalk
and the buds start to swell.   The flowers, that
are the size and a shape of a half eggshell, are
waxy in appearance and prove very attractive to
the bees.   The evening breeze blows a delicate
fragrance from the bells and they gleam a luminous

white in the twilight.

Larkspur, the annual in this group, will be mentioned in another chapter, so I will say only that I leave a few of the volunteer plants until they have scattered seed and then remove the spent plants from the garden.

Beautiful, double hollyhocks are better treated as biennials and replaced each year. Their seeds will not produce plants like their parents, but revert to a single type of bloom. It is better to start new plants when the old ones lose their vigor.

Dictamnus is slow to establish itself, but is a very interesting plant once it decides that it likes the location you gave it. It needs at least half a day of sunlight and good, deep soil as its roots are very long. It needs ample water and good drainage. It has very attractive leaves and spikes of pink or white flowers that attain a height of three feet or so. The flowers give off a very sweet odor, but it is not noticeable unless you are standing very close to the plant. On warm evenings when there is no breeze, a lighted match held close to the top of a paper cone held over the blooms lights a tiny burst of flame. This does not happen too often. When the flowers fade and drop, a very unusual looking group of seed pods is left. These dry well and make a very welcome addition to the dried plant material cache.

Several of the campanulas produce attractive bells on spikes of various heights. Veronica blooms in late May and June. This is followed by lavender, lythrum and liatris all with myriads of tiny, brightly colored flowers.

Lythrum, dictamnus, lupines and veronica disappear completely during the winter. The others show green clumps of various sizes to mark their places. Delphiniums and foxglove must be staked to keep them from being blown down by the winds.

Why not add a few more to your perennial bed for next year?

GOING TO WORK ON IRIS BEDS

Every time I have to work over one of my
iris beds, I am thankful for several things.

- The job can be spread over two or three
  days
- If necessary, rhyzomes may be stored
  for a week or two after digging –
  they should be placed in a cool spot
  if planting is postponed
- Work can be staggered so that one bed
  can be done one year, another the
  next and so forth until all the beds
  are done
- Four years is the average time between
  periods of working over an iris bed

Digging up an iris bed may be started as
early as mid–July or delayed until early August.
Ample time should be allowed for the newly set out
plants to become established before cold weather
sets in. The first thing to do after digging out
the iris plants is to mark each one so that its
name and color won't be lost. A Rub-a-Dub pen
works beautifully for this as one can use it to
write the name and color on each plant low down
on a leaf.

Leaves should be trimmed so that a five
or six inch fan is left on each rhyzome. The part
of the rhyzome which has the remains of a stalk
on it – one that has bloomed – should be thrown
away. It will not bloom again. So should the
older part of the rhyzome which is now useless.

The rhyzomes that are ready to be transplanted should be laid aside in a shed or other
protected place while one is working over the bed.
If the soil shows any sign of disease or for any
other reason is not suitable, it should be replaced.
Otherwise, turn over the soil well, remove all
weeds that are evident, add compost and a few
handfuls of superphosphate (0-20-0) and mix it in
well. I also add some commercial potting soil to

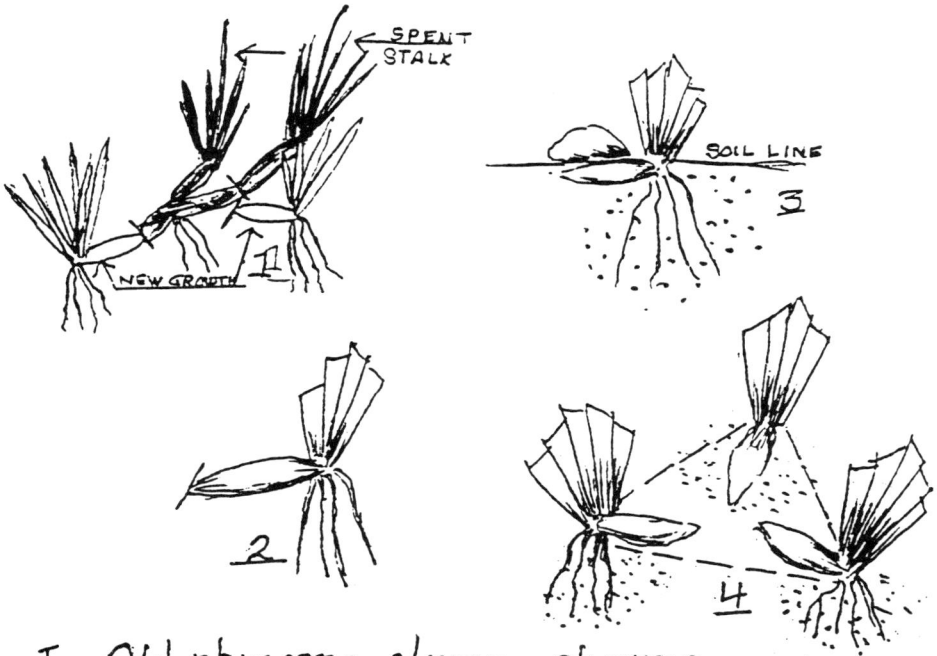

1 Old rhizome clump. showing
old and new growth. Arrows point to old
bloom stalks which must be discarded.

2. New rhizome ready for planting. Leaves
are trimmed to 5 inches. Rhyzome has been
cut neatly from old clump.

3. Rhizome planted correctly. Roots tucked
deep in soil mixed with 0-20-0. Rhyzome is
laid flat and barely covered with soil Brick or
stone holds it securely until established.

4. Plant in triangles—toes in and leaves out.

the mix.

Ideally, iris rhyzomes should be planted in a triangle 12 to 15 inches on each side. The fans should form the corners of the triangle and the rhyzomes should point toward the center. Tuck the roots down deep into the soil, but lay the rhyzomes flat with only about an inch of soil over them. Pieces of brick or stones laid over the rhyzomes will keep them steady until the plants have anchored themselves in the earth. I leave them on all winter as protection against our uncertain weather and pets wandering around in the flower beds.

Iris should be planted where there is always good drainage and where watering can be curtailed after they have bloomed. Like Oriental poppies, they want very little water after their blooming period is over. However, after transplanting, they should be watered regularly until they have become established.

As I have said before, superphosphate (0-20-0) should be worked into the soil at planting time. This slow-acting fertilizer will feed the plants until it is time to divide them again. However, each spring, well before blooming time, a generous side dressing of steer (not horse) manure should be spread around the plants and watered in well. Watch out for leaf miners and at the first sign of their trails along the leaves, spray with malathion to remedy the problem. Don't be disappointed if some of your iris plants do not bloom the first year. Some iris plants take more time to become established.

8. SELF SEEDING ANNUALS

May is the time for planting most annuals, but there are a few that you can plant for color in your garden a little later in the year. Some annuals do not transplant well, and in such cases it is better to do your own planting at the proper time.

Much help is given by Mother Nature who has supplied certain plants with the happy faculty of re-seeding themselves. Among these are California poppies, larkspur, bachelor buttons, bells of Ireland, snow-on-the-mountain, calendulas, dwarf marigolds and anchusa.

Besides offering a beautiful and prolonged burst of color, starting with the California poppies and ending when the autumn frost finally claims the last of the calendulas and marigolds, many of these plants supply food for our seed-eating friends. These little visitors will bring a note of cheer, whether they stop by on their way south, or brave the winter months counting on some bounty from their human friends.

Many years ago the service station at which I traded gave me several packets of wild flower seeds. The first year brought a profusion of attractive wild flowers to an otherwise almost barren garden plot. As the years went by, all the other plants joined the ranks of the drop-outs, but the California poppies persist year after year with a splash of gold here and there among the other plants.

Larkspur continually re-seeds from my first planting many years ago. The bachelor buttons are more or less confined to an area near the house, and are encouraged in areas so placed that the wild canaries can see the cats approaching and fly to safety. Bright blue and pale pink flowers splash the grey-green foliage with color.

The bells of Ireland which someone gave me long ago, have spread their progeny far and wide. The winds and the birds have carried the seed to the adjoining vacant lots where a wet spring encourages the growth of many of these attractive plants. The interesting shape of the bells, their delicate coloring when dried, and the gracefully arching branches make them excellent for dried arrangements.

A few snow-on-the-mountain plants, which my uncle gave me many years ago, have so multiplied that their descendants have numbered thousands. This member of the euphorbias is one of my favorite annuals for it makes a striking accent plant. It re-seeds very profusely, so after giving away plants to those who wish them, I pull out the extra ones. The very few left in the flower beds grow to two feet in height with graceful branches that spread that much in width. The white margined leaves enhance the many-colored flowers that grow among them. On moonlit nights they shine like shimmering silver from late July until the plants go to seed and then dry.

A few calendulas which I brought home from a friend's garden filled one of the small flower beds during their first year. They have spread their seeds in the neighboring flower beds so a carpet of many petalled blooms, ranging from pale yellow to a deep red-orange come back every year for a bright spot that lasts until Jack Frost decides to pick them in late fall. The dwarf marigolds will self-sow successfully if you provide a place in the sun for them. Like the calendulas, they last until frost and transplant easily. They make attractive, low-growing borders, are neat and compact, and their foliage is very attractive. Their pungent odor is said to repel aphids, so a place for them near plants that are prone to host aphids, is desirable.

I can hear a few of you saying, "These annuals will take over and become a weed". Not so, because a once-over with the scuffle hoe will remove all unwanted plants in a jiffy. Those growing too closely among other flowers, can be removed once they are tall enough to grasp. An annual once removed, will not return. They are not like perennial spreaders that must be watched so they will not usurp the areas intended for other plants.

Because of the amount of time involved in starting plants from seed and caring for them, I prefer buying my annuals in flats or by the dozens. Each year, I buy petunias, asters, and a few African or French marigolds. Sometimes I buy zinnias, and sometimes I sow these outdoors since they are easily started in their permanent home when the soil is warmed by the sun. Get your plants locally whenever possible. I don't buy plants until they have been in Reno for several days. Then I place the flats on my planting bench and give them a good drenching with a root stimulating solution and plan to plant them the next day.

Under usual spring conditions, I put my annuals out in late May. A bundle of shingles, which lasts for several years, is used to make A-frames over the young plants until they have become established in their new homes. Remember to pinch off the tops of your annuals when they are about five or six inches tall. This will encourage side branches to shoot out and make for a more attractive, bushier, and more floriferous plant. Be sure you pinch a quarter of an inch above a leaf or leaf cluster. New shoots come from the axil of the leaves just under the place where you pinched off the tip of the stem.

9. THIS AND THAT

Many gardeners think that all plants have blooms that last for several days before fading. However, that is not so. There are several one-day bloomers that add much to the beauty of the flower garden. Best known of these is no doubt, the day lily. This attractive perennial, only a decade or so ago was usually seen only as a tall-growing plant which sported many buds that over succeeding days burst out in orange lilies that bloomed for only one day.

Hybridizers have done much with this attractive plant. Among the many improvements, day lilies have developed much larger blooms, in many cases shorter stems that make them more useful in narrower borders, broader leaves and many colors. The array of colors is amazing - off whites through the yellows, orange and apricot tones, pinks, rose tones, reds both bright and deeper toned, petals of one color tinted deep in the throat with another. Even purple tones can be detected in some. Only blue is missing from this galaxy of colors.

Besides, several of these plants have a double row of petals. Several send up second bloom stalks during the growing season - the second cluster of blooms as attractive as the first.

Anchusa, whose coarse, hairy leaves encircle the lower part of the plant is topped by hundreds of bright blue flowers. It is covered every morning with these bright blue blooms that fade toward evening only to make way for hundreds more the following day. It produces a colorful accent in the flower border, and when all the blooms are spent, the tall stalks may be cut back to about a foot. In time new shoots will bring forth another crop of blooms.

Smaller in size, but no less attractive is the perennial spiderwort. The leaves are strap-like as are those of the day lily, but the growth pattern is different. These plants appreciate dappled shade and are happy in most flower borders. Atop each stalk there appears a cluster of small, tear-drop shaped buds, each of which blooms for one day only, but on successive days more appear until the whole cluster has bloomed. Spiderwort may be had in several colors - white, white with a blue eye, blue, magenta and purple. Larger, older plants may be divided in the spring.

A rose that blooms only one day? Yes, that's the butterfly rose whose real name is Rosa chinensis mutabilis. The bush is of medium size, many-branched and covered with foliage that has overtones of red. The buds are numerous, several to each cluster on the many canes. Each five-petaled bloom opens a clear yellow and during the course of the day goes through gradual changes so that by late afternoon it is a deep rose color. Since the blooms open at different times during the day, several colors appear on the bush at any given time. The bush is very attractive against a wooden fence or an evergreen backdrop.

Another one-day bloomer is the shrub Potentilla fructicosa. Originally these shrubs came in yellow only - as does mine - but in later years new ones have been hybridized so that red is playing an important part in the color changes. The bush starts blooming in early June, the nickel-sized, five-petaled flowers covering the entire bush. Hundreds of buds nestled on each branch wait their turn as those of the preceding day drop to the ground below. This shrub is happier when it is in dappled shade during the hotter hours of the summer.

Perhaps the most spectacular of the plants that bear flowers that bloom for only a day is the hibiscus Moscheutos palustris. This beauty comes in many colors in the white, pink, rose and red tones. The blooms are huge - ten to twelve inches

across. The deciduous bush itself attains tremendous size, shooting up each spring from the ground
to a height of four feet and a span of five feet in
breadth. It does well in full sun and requires
sufficient space so that it can spread to its full
size. Also, it requires ample water as its species
name (palustris - meaning growing in a swamp or
marsh) indicates. However, my two which have
good drainage do very well. Many buds grow at
the end of each stalk and a succession of blooms
through July and into part of August make these
plants very worth while for any garden. A word
of warning to the prospective buyer. If you wish
to have one or more of these plants for your
garden, select the site carefully. The tremendous
root system will be hard to move if you change
your mind about the location.

     Now comes an unusual specimen for our
location. It's a tree whose blooms last only one
day; it is borderline here and in some parts of
Reno will not survive the winter. The tree
Albizia julibrissin commonly known as floss silk
tree will grow to forty feet in climates to which it
is better suited. In Reno, at twenty feet, it is
considered almost full-grown. The tree branches
out into a wide canopy and leaves like those of a
locust clothe it abundantly. The blooms, pink-
tipped tassels two inches across appear in clusters. They are sweet-smelling and especially
attractive to humming birds. Each evening the
spent blooms fade and drop to be replaced by new
ones the following day.

THE COLOR BLUE BRIGHTENS GARDENS FOR

MANY MONTHS

     Blue can do wonders for a flower garden.
From early spring through September, blue blooms
intermingled with other colors will present a con-
tinual show for the gardener.

     Grape hyacinths, several different scillas

and glory of the snow greet the early spring,
followed very quickly by triteleias and blue hyacinths. Then come larkspur and delphinium, the
latter which will bloom again if the spent stalks
are removed. Camassias, almost two feet tall,
bloom early, and their blue spikes lend happy
accents to the garden.

Bell flower, early and late-blooming kinds,
round out the spring and summer seasons. Bright
blue anchusa and blue flax open their eyes each
morning only to close them forever at night, but
greet us again the next day with another burst of
bloom from new buds.

Then there are the many iris types. The
tiny ones are the earliest bloomers. Although
they come in many colors, the blues among them
are many, ranging from light blues through the
medium and darker tones.

The intermediate group is next to bloom.
Not as well known nor as popular as the bearded
giants, nevertheless they make a spectacular show
if planted by themselves, so they are not dwarfed
by their larger relatives. Here, too, one may find
a number of them in blues: light, medium and
dark.

The most spectacular of these are the
bearded iris - the giants of the iris world. Some
attain a height of over three feet, while others,
though not as tall, still boast blooms of tremendous size. The blues among these are myriad -
light, medium, dark, icy or tinged with different
degrees of warmth, depending on the amount of
warm color added to their basic makeup. There
are selfs (one color), amoenas (blue falls and
white standards), plicatas (blue-edged falls with
standards usually of one color) and neglectas (two
shades of the same color). And then there are
the beards of many colors to add interest to each
bloom. They come in white, blue, yellow, orange
and red - all to add to the array of colors of the
blooms themselves.

Nor should one forget the Siberian and

Dutch iris. Both are daintier than those previously mentioned, have long, slender leaves and smaller blooms set on shorter stems. Again, one will find several different blooms in these categories.

Sage, both the annual and perennial types, has spikes of deep blue blooms that last for a long time in the summer garden. Blue mist, a shrub attaining a height of two feet or so, is clothed in masses of blue florets in July and August. This shrub must be pruned severely each spring if it is to do its best. Columbines may also be found in blues and make an interesting contrast when planted among those of other colors. So, too, will blue lupines, whose tall spikes make interesting garden specimens. Stokes aster and Liriope add two different blues and flower forms to the flower beds.

Forget-me-nots, a perennial with tiny blue petals and bright yellow eyes, greet the spring scene and add interest to the flower bed or border. Among the annuals, ageratum and lobelia also make attractive borders for the beds.

One finds larkspur in both light and darker blues, and the dainty creeper, verbena. Salvia and pincushion flower in both annual and perennial types do their share in making a beautiful blue world.

Plumbago spreads a lovely green carpet in shade or semishade. In late summer, from a bed of foliage six to eight inches tall, brilliant blue flowers about the size of a dime pop up in great numbers. These persist through the fall with an added bonus in bright copper-colored leaves when autumn nights turn cold.

This is not a complete list of the blue flowers that will grow in our area, but it will give you some suggestions. Because most of these mentioned are perennials, the problem of yearly planting is eliminated. The many different sizes, types, growth habits and seasons during which they bloom will keep blues in the garden all season long.

WHENCE DID THEY COME?

We rarely stop to think that among people we know are those who are from other places and whose fathers have crossed oceans and plains to make their homes among us. Somehow, somewhere, in the move from their native homes great changes in their way of living have taken place, and many major adjustments have had to be made. They have learned new skills, a new language, and have learned to adjust to different environments. They have merged into the general surroundings with few ripples as they took their places among those already here. They came of their own volition from necessity, because of adverse conditions else-where, or to find better homes.

Have you ever stopped to think which plants in your garden were at one time strangers to our area? They have come here not of their own will, but because someone chose to try them out in a new environment. Olive trees from Spain and grapes from Italy found their way to California with immigrants who sought to carry some of their homeland with them. Rhubarb came to us from Europe, where it found its way during the Crusades, having been brought from the near East to spread all over the western world. Spices and herbs from the far and near East, and other regions where they were used as preservatives as well as flavoring, are well-known to many of us today.

Besides those plants that have become naturalized, many have failed to adapt to our locale. Heat, cold, extreme changes of temperature, altitude, humidity, soil conditions and other factors in the new surroundings proved, and continue to prove insurmountable to many specimens. They have fallen by the wayside and have not been heard of by the general public.

Many plants do make the grade. Selection of the right spot, the proper shelter, remedies to combat their enemies, suitable soil and

water conditions and winter protection have helped many specimens to adapt themselves to our area.
Coupled with a strong consitutition, and given
more than ordinary care, many imports live and
thrive for us.

Besides plants whose forebears have been
in our location for a long time, I have in my garden several first generation plants representative
of many gardening friends and various regions.
Some are common here, others less so, as they
require special care and more attention than most
people care to devote to them.

I have two silk trees (Albizia julibrissin).
One was purchased, but the other came from seed
given me by a friend who brought the pods here
from her mother's Staten Island home. One of the
trees blooms with bright pink tassels perched in
clusters above the lacy leaves. The other one
gets less sunlight. As it grows older and taller,
it will receive sunlight for a longer period of time
and then will start to bloom.

A fern which I brought down from the
high Sierras has lived with us for over forty years.
Though several others did not survive, this one,
first placed under a leaky water tap lived for
twenty years in its first Reno home. When it was
moved to a special acid corner in my present garden, it took advantage of the more suitable environment and spread so that I have been able to
make several new plants from it.

Two filbert trees which friends sent me
from Oregon have indicated that they do not like
our hot, drying air and need lots of water to keep
them happy. A location where they are shaded by
larger objects, and an abundance of water has
caused them to respond to the special treatment.
They even bear a few filberts each year.

Marsh iris from its former home in Vermont
have multiplied and greet each spring with their
tiny yellow blooms on slender stems. They love
water, so they have been planted by the pool and
in another spot which receives ample water to keep

them happy.

Gunnera is a long way from its original home off the coast of Chile, but it is happy in the shade of larger trees by the pool and it receives the extra moisture it craves when the begonias and fuchsias get their daily sprinkling. It loves our high altitude and can stand our cold winter climate. Huge clumps of it can also be found along the Yuba River and other spots in the Sierra.

The princess flower, originally from Brazil, came to my garden by way of San Francisco. To simulate that moist atmosphere, I place it in the dappled shade of the birch tree in summer, where it receives frequent mistings with the hose, and rewards me during the cooler days of fall by bursting forth with gorgeous purple velvet flowers that sport wickedly interesting stamens. It spends its winters in the cold greenhouse where it is happy and sometimes surprises me with an off-season bloom or two.

A California friend gave me my first shrimp plant (Beloperone guttata). It has done beautifully over the years, and many new plants started from it have found homes in other indoor gardens during the winter and in the half-shade of shrubs during the summer. Mexico and Hawaii both claim the plant as theirs, but whatever the origin, it has made many friends far from its native home.

The royal poinciana, sometimes called bird of paradise bush, but in no way related to the Strelitzia reginae, lives in the warm corner that I call my sub-tropical plant bed. When a friend gave me the little seedling only about ten inches high I never dreamed that it would give so much pleasure over the years. It attained eight feet in height and the recurved yellow petals that encase the long red tassel-like anthers cover the tops of the branches. It is really too tender for our area and a great deal of the wood is winter-killed during a severe winter. A recent winter

proved the worst one.   Only one of the trunks
survived and that had to be cut to less than two
feet in height.   New growth rose to about three
feet high, and I hope it will bloom again for many
years.   It's worth all the worry as the thermometer drops lower and lower and stays there for
days on end.   If the intense cold does not last
too long, and the damage is not too severe, then
the following May little shoots greet another spring.

The newest additions to my unusual plants
are two plumerias which came from Hawaii.   I was
delighted to receive them.   They spent the first
winter indoors, and late in the spring I placed
them into larger containers and moved them to the
cold greenhouse, where they sent forth many
glossy new leaves.   When they return to their
winter home in the living room, or perhaps my
bedroom, they are placed in one of the large metal
planters with the clerodendrons.   The pots stand
on bricks and the water level is kept just below
the bottoms of the pots.   Evaporation of the water
gives the air around the plants moisture to simulate, as much as possible, the atmospheric conditions of their native home.   The plants are subject to white flies indoors and a constant vigil
with the spray can or a systemic should be used
to remedy the situation.

As you have noticed, the dryness of our
area and the wide range of temperature during a
twenty-four hour period, our unpredictable winters and very hot summers are the principal problems with many of our plants from other regions.
However, if you are willing to take the time and
can provide a space where you can attempt to
simulate the environment of their native homes,
you might like to try a few exotics.   Their performance can be rewarding.

10. PROBLEM SOLVERS

It was a lucky spring day when I walked to the mailbox, and on the way saw my neighbor getting ready to run a power rake on his lawn. He guided the rake over a small area, and as I watched the dead grass and thatch rise behind it, I knew that the power rake was the answer to my problem.

The beautiful lawn that had surrounded the house when it was first built had long since acquired many uninvited additions. Dandelions, dock, shepherd's purse and plantains from the near-by fields had sent their little air-borne seeds to plague us. Loads of manure which had been brought in to add humus brought other seeds with them. Crabgrass found its way into the lawns and the flower beds. Several years later when we seeded the last barren expanse in the lower yard, it too, became the victim of unwelcome intruders.

Much of what had happened to the lawns was our fault. Too many times we had mowed without using the grass catcher. This helped produce a deep thatch that prevented penetration of water and fertilizer, smothered grass roots and formed a fine bed for new weed seeds.

The idea of tearing up the entire lawn area, bringing in new soil, rolling it smooth and replanting - not to mention the long hours that must be spent sprinkling a newly seeded lawn at intervals, was more than I cared to face. So one morning I drove down to the rental agency to pick up a power rake. The man at the agency gave me the necessary basic instructions on running the machine. Then he motioned with his hand as he said, "All you have to do is run it this way across the lawn, and then run it that way. Then you rake up the stuff that it pulls out."

I must have picked the right day for that job. A young friend was in town and volunteered to run the rake around the yard for a few laps. He must have enjoyed doing it, or perhaps he figured that it would probably take me a week to complete the job, for he did the entire area. Not once this way and that way - as the man at the rental agency had said - but repeatedly the power rake was run over each area. Billows of thatch and dead grasses crested in the wake of the machine as it went back and forth. I had a hard time raking and removing the debris fast enough to clear the path for the next time around. One would not have imagined how much had accumulated over the past seasons. Over a pick-up truck load of waste was removed. Several areas that had been taken over by crabgrass were bare as the dead crabgrass was torn away. The rest of the lawn was bare indeed, tracks of the blades showed everywhere, and as we laughingly remarked, there was a bald lawn.

The following day I measured out the correct amount of urea which is a high nitrogen fertilizer. I didn't take time to find the spreader, but put on a pair of gloves and spread it by hand. I watered the lawn according to directions, and the waiting began. In a short while, deep swirls of lush green grass appeared. In between were barren areas that indicated that the hand spreading of the urea was not evenly done.

In a short while when the heavier lawn growth was well defined, I fertilized again. This time I concentrated on the areas that had not received fertilizer before. The lawn responded, and by summer's end was thick and heavy.

In the meantime, upon advice from the Washoe County Extension Service, the areas that had been stripped of crabgrass had new soil added and were newly seeded. The blades of the lawn mower were raised, and deep watering days apart, replaced the shallower, more frequent waterings. Thus crabgrass met its three worst natural enemies - shady areas around weed seeds that need light and heat to develop, fertilized lawn that produced heavy turf which impeded the progress of crab grass, and watering at longer intervals that cut down the moisture around the thirsty pest.

The power rake did not remove the dandelions, plantains, dock and other broad-leafed weeds. These receive periodic doses of a herbicide designed for them and applied with a long green tube. More often, when I have the time, a long-handled weed remover is used, the sharp-pronged tip reaching deep into the soil to remove the roots as well as the tops of the weeds. Removing the heads of these weeds before they mature also prevents the sowing of new plants through the distribution of seeds.

The lawn isn't new again, but almost so. Had I been aware that the power rake could do so much, the work would have been done much sooner. Thus we could have enjoyed a nicer lawn much longer. Too, thanks to the extension agent's suggestion, four half strength feedings spaced at shorter intervals will replace the customary two feedings a year for the lawn. This will make for a more even growth during the coming seasons.

Another word - if you use the highly soluble urea as a fertilizer, don't leach it away by drowning your lawn after applying it. Water it in only to root depth - four or five inches. And remember that a 45% fertilizer is very potent. Better too little than too much.

THE OLDER YARD

A number of years ago an instructor from whom I was taking a summer school course half-jokingly remarked that freshmen should be well scared by their teachers. His reason was that if the freshmen were made to realize immediately that college was no joke, they would get down to business and be better students during the ensuing years.

As I wrote about a new yard for a new home I thought of that remark and its application to new gardeners. This chapter is for those of us who did not get scared soon enough and well enough to avoid many of the pitfalls waiting for us as we plan our yards. (Yes, I too was one of them). Then there are those among us who have fallen heir to yards planned by others and that came to us with ideas that are not our own.

Are you one of those who have too many shrubs? Are some of your larger plants too close to the sidewalk or the foundation of the house? Is there a tall shrub or tree in front of a window blocking the view? Does your neighbor's yard drain into yours or vice-versa? Have you noticed that a certain vine seems to have suddenly become a hopeless tangle of branches? Do you want a fence placed somewhere or one removed? Any of the situations mentioned can be better remedied in the fall, leaving your spring days free for work on your herbacious perennials and the general cleanup that follows winter storms.

Let's start with the too plentiful shrubs and evergreen trees. That first early, unseasonable cold has probably induced dormancy by now, so they can be moved to a new location. Perhaps you have a friend or two to whom you can give extras. A good garden book will give you directions for digging them up carefully and moving them safely to a new location. Several years ago friends moved my six-foot Norway spruce so it would be farther from the fence I was erecting. They anchored it securely with posts and ropes which I removed the following season. They also moved four shrubs, and three of them are doing well today. The other one did not survive and that was because I forgot to water it well as it was adjusting to its new location. The spruce?

It's over forty feet tall.

Young deciduous trees are better moved in late February or early March, but there is no reason why the holes cannot be prepared now. That shrub that may eventually damage the foundation, those that are spreading over the walk and the tall ones that obstruct the view from your windows should be removed outright. Do it now and when spring comes you will be ready with other plans for those spots.

Build a raised bed if drainage from your neighbor's yard is a problem. Or perhaps a drain may be the answer. Or if you can afford the space, why not get the spot ready for a planting of bamboo or reeds next spring? Either of these require ample water and the spot would be ideal. I use the canes to make supports for dahlias and other tall plants. On the other hand, if you flood your neighbor's yard, why not talk matters over with him and work out a compatible solution.

Now, let's get at the vines. Since most of the leaves are gone you can follow the branches as they twist in and out. Mark those you wish to remove by tying a twistem (one of those green wire ties) at the spot where you wish to sever the offender. Then with a spray can, color the branch here and there so you will be able to follow it through the tangle and cut at different places where necessary to make removal easier. Honeysuckle vines do not drop too many leaves, but enough fall so you can see the tangle of dead twigs that will not leaf out again. Cut these off with your clippers and pull out the mass, being careful not to injure your hands. You will have a clean, airy vine ready for spring.

If you have a fence to consider it is a good time to do it when herbaceous perennials are dormant and not so easily damaged by trampling feet. A plank laid across a sleeping perennial bed will protect the plants while you are working and can be removed easily when the work is done.

Now if you will review the suggestions

made for the people with new yards you will find
that many of them can be applied to your yard.
So much of this heavier work can be done now
instead of waiting for our uncertain spring weather, and the really "fun" part of gardening will
not have to be postponed until the necessary
major tasks are done.

HOLD BACK THE HILL

A sudden torrent of rain can make us
realize that repeated bursts of heavy rains will
soon wear away the earth, creating gullies and
ditches. These will in time remove much of the
good earth in our yards and leave gaping holes
that must be filled, or it will be easier for later
rainstorms and melting snow to do more damage.

Retaining wall must be
set on a firm foundation.
Top of wall should
be higher than top
of earth behind it.

Cement footing
covered with soil.

earth
below top of
wall.

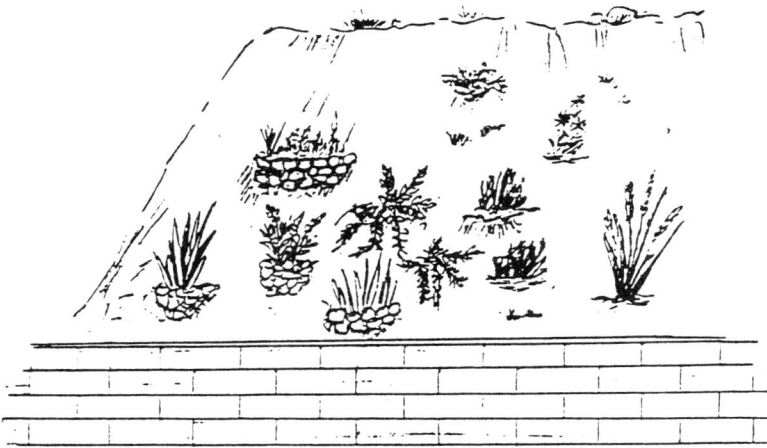

If you are one of those homeowners who
have a barren hill overlooking your lot and threatening to come down upon you as an avalanche, or
have a slope in front of your house that is grad-
ually washing away part of your yard, it is well
to consider a remedy for the situation. No time
is better than during the spring or early fall.
Perhaps you have much ground work to do before
setting in plants. Gullies should be filled, rocks
moved to a place where they will do some good.
weeds removed and perhaps, a number of terraces
made.

Consider your situation before you get
into the actual work. If you have a slope directly behind your lot, it is probably just above a
wall or barricade which was set up to keep the

slope from taking over your yard. In many cases it is much too low to do the job permanently because the storms of past seasons have filled in the space behind it with soil that has washed down. Leveling off this first area a few feet back will make an excellent first terrace on which to plant shrubs that will hang over the wall. It will relieve that stark bareness, and afford a network of roots that will hold the soil firmly. Creeping cotoneaster and juniper are excellent for this purpose, and when fully established will need only a minimum of care and an occasional haircut if they venture too far over the wall.

If there are rocks on the slope, select a large one that is firmly set, make a pocket behind it, and surround it with other rocks to make a small terrace. Do this all over making use of all rocks that are securely anchored as a base for each little terrace. Place bulbs to the front so they can be seen from your windows and you can enjoy the beauty and practicality of your labors. Behind the bulbs, plant a perennial that will bloom later in the season. Select plants that produce a heavy network of roots. Among these are veronica, various perennial daisies, Michaelmas daisies, lythrum and physostegia. The height of Michaelmas daisies can be controlled by cutting them back when they are within two or three inches of the desired height. Among the terraces, place ground covers and low growing plants. Creeping phlox will brighten the hillside in spring. Sedums will spread all over during the summer. Rockcress, lamb's ears, bishop's weed and St. John's wort will bloom at different times and keep your hillside interesting as well as practical. Some of these plants will do without too much watering. Perhaps if you have a neighbor at the top of the hill who leaves the water running on his lawn all day, the seepage may be enough to take care of the watering at the top of the slope. A hose placed here and there with a sprinkler attached will take care of the rest of the watering easily.

Then, as the small plants become larger and larger, they take over and the entire hill is covered with vegetation. A man I know planted squash vines and cucumbers on his backyard slope. Since that location gets sun almost all day, his gardening has been very successful.

If your front yard slopes too much for a lawn to be practical, try planting it with ajuga, creeping phlox, aubrieta, rockcress and other creepers. These are spring bloomers which can be placed among later blooming plants. They will need attention from time to time as they tend to spread, but they will cover the ground well and be worth the time necessary for their upkeep. It may be well to arrange rocks along the top of the slope. Others may be placed here and there all over the slope to provide an anchor for the plants. Bulbs tucked in among the rocks will brighten the area in spring. If watering is a problem, hens and chickens and sedums are the answer. They do well with little or no water when well established, and will do well with what little rain falls and an occasional sprinkling with the hose. They will grow larger and more quickly with more water and will not be damaged if there is good drainage.

Rome wasn't built in a day. Neither will your terracing be done in a day. But do start now. Lay your basic pattern, and little by little, keep adding to it. Extra plants from your garden, from your friends and neighbors and the local nurseries will make a beauty spot of which you will be very proud. I have not mentioned all the possibilities - but just the suitable plants that grow in my own yard. Look around, study your flower catalogs and ask questions. You will become enthused and the project will be well on its way. And, best of all, these sudden downpours will no longer cause concern.

11. THE ACID GARDEN

My acid garden spot is as much the result of accident as it is of design. I'd always wanted a rhododendron bush, and during a trip to Oregon I found that they were partial to shade, disliked wind, and needed moisture.

When the house was built, I realized that the northeast side receives sunshine only during the early part of the day. Two louvred extensions, one at each end, parry the wind. The area is close to a water tap, and, thanks to the shadow cast by the house, can be watered at almost any time of the day.

Making the soil acid was the first task. Much of the heavy clay soil was removed and replaced with a loamy type which was then spaded into the clay so the two were more or less thoroughly mixed. Sulphur was added to the soil as directed on the package, and a bale of peat moss was mixed in with the rest.

Of three rhododendrons which I planted originally, one has survived, does well, and brings home a ribbon each time it sends a representative to the flower show. Mars is its name, it is small and spreading in character, only four an a half feet tall, and the clusters of flowers are a true red.

Very soon the rhododendrons had company. I planted laurel at the southeast corner, and despite two or three bad winters, it now reaches the eves of the house. Nestling close to it are Mr. and Mrs. gold dust plant (Aucuba). The male tree is sheltered by the laurel and is larger and more robust than its mate that gets a little too much sun, and shows traces of sunburn. A hydrangea joined them some time later, but the winters keep it small, as it suffers from a certain amount of winter-kill each year.

The bed stayed this way for three or four years. In the winter I collected discarded Christmas trees from friends and laid them gently over the young shrubs. They gave the necessary protection from heavy snow, yet allowed air and light to reach the plants. As winter progressed, the needles from the Christmas trees dropped, scattering an acid mulch over the bed.

About this time, I discovered a ground bark soil conditioner, and a sackful is added to the bed every two or three years. It is carefully worked in, as the roots of these plants are very shallow.

One day, I went to see a friend's garden. In it was a lovely Hydrangea quercifolia. Nothing would do but I must have one, so at the first opportunity I bought one and placed it in the middle of the bed. It is a lovely, robust plant with leaves similar to those of an oak, and it leafs out early enough to keep the colors of red Mars and a later addition, blue-red Americana, from screaming at each other when they are in bloom. Three Exbury azaleas complete the list of shrubs in this bed, which is less than four feet wide.

Besides the woody shrubs, a number of other plants have a home in the acid garden. Bishop's weed and myrtle cover part of the surface area. A fern which has been with us for over thirty years finds a shelter under the laurel, and two divisions from it are also in the same bed. A start of Japanese anemone which was given to me several springs ago sends tall stems high above its beautiful leaves and blooms all summer long. A clump of hosta from another garden shows its white and green leaves behind one of the rhododendrons.

Several years ago, when I purchased more Oriental poppy plants than I had room for, I put one in a bare spot in that bed, only temporarily - I thought. But the poppy has been very happy there, so two friends joined it lately.

However, I avoid sprinkling sulphur in the vicinity of these plants, and since I no longer cover the bed with evergreens in December, no more needles fall to produce an acid mulch. A little manure around the poppies keeps them happy, and they produce their share of colorful flowers. I also avoid fertilizing them when the shrubs are fed with a commercial fertilizer.

The plants in this bed are mostly shallow-rooted and must be watered frequently. A deep mulch of ground bark helps to retain moisture in the earth and makes it easy to remove any foolish little weed that dares raise its head in that overgrown area.

It is best to buy shrubs for an acid bed in the spring, but they will be grateful for prepparation of your soil in the fall. It will give time for the various substances to act and produce a humusy, acid bed.

12. SPRING AND FALL FAVORITES

The period of time from mid-August to the end of the month is best for transplanting Oriental poppies in this area. A few simple rules will ensure a successful planting of these exotic beauties.

Like most early blooming perennials, they want a place in the sun. Good drainage is necessary because once they have made their spectacular show they are ready to rest. Excess moisture during the rest of the season will be detrimental to them. It is wise to plan a place for them where watering is easily controlled, because after the blooms are gone, all they want is enough water to keep the roots from drying up. I should make a note here. Raspberry Queen is one of the most beautiful specimens and should be planted in a location where it receives only an hour or two of direct morning sun.

Well-established plants have roots that grow deep into the earth; hence, it is necessary to prepare a bed to a depth of a foot or more. I have dug up plants that had roots so long that they broke off when I moved them. A year or so later, part of the root left in the soil found its way to the surface and a new plant appeared where I had dug one out. However, all roots are not that large. Raspberry Queen, which will sport stems four feet or more in height, produces one of the smallest roots among these plants.

A long time ago I read that pieces of Oriental poppy roots about three inches long will produce a plant if they are laid horizontally in a well-prepared bed, covered to a depth of three inches and kept moist during the growing season. I had occasion to try this when a friend gave me pieces of roots which were supposed to be of

Rajah, a gorgeous red poppy. They came up and bloomed. However, it was not Rajah that came up, but a lovely salmon pink. (I have no longer been able to find Rajah on the market.)

When preparing to dig Oriental poppy roots, water the area well the day before so digging will be easier. Prepare the new spot by digging deeply, adding compost and the fertilizer superphosphate (0-20-0) and working them well into the soil. If you are going to use one of the old spots again, it is wise to replace the soil with a good garden loam to which compost and superphosphate (0-20-0) have been added.

Hold the spade straight up and drive it deeply into the earth. Lift out the root or roots and shake off the soil. If the roots have sprouted leaves, trim them off to about two inches in length. If they have not sprouted any, that's all right. They will sprout leaves as soon as they become established. If some of the larger roots are funnel-shaped, that is, they have a hole in them reaching into the depth of the root, cut a V-shaped notch into the root so that water will not collect in the cut. Dust the cut with agricultural sulfur or diazinon dust and allow to callus for an hour or so before planting.

Bury the root with the top three inches under the surface of the soil. Water with a solution of plant starter hormone, cover the area with leafy branches to ward off the hot sun and keep the earth moist. Most plants will sprout leaf clusters this fall, but even if they don't, they will send them up next spring. If you are in a location where quail and other birds nip off the tops of your plants, place inverted strawberry baskets on them and fasten them securely with bamboo stakes.

CHRYSANTHEMUMS

Frost has seared the garden another time. The cold nights have taken their toll of all but

the hardiest. A few roses still vie for the title
of "last rose of summer." The petunias that were
well protected by larger growth and the verbenas
nestled in the flower box in front of the house
still persist. The Michaelmas daisies are a blaze
of pink, purple and fuchsia, but all else has felt
the cold breath of approaching winter.

Now the chrysanthemums come into their
own. Their gorgeous colors, the warm hues of
autumn will last for some time to come. They
appear in many colors - white, shades of yellow,
orange, red, copper, bronze, rose and purple.
They also come in bicolor combinations that challenge the imagination. Only blue seems to be
missing from this array.

As different as their colors are the varieties obtainable to suit your fancy. Early types
that bloom in mid-August through the late-blooming
types that last far into November are available.
Cushion mums of various types form flower-covered
mounds up to almost two feet in height and breadth.
Button chrysanthemums, their saucy little pompoms
ablaze with color, bloom in October. Tall single
flowering types that resemble daisies come in
bright colors on long graceful stems.

The regular garden mums produce beautiful sprays and the larger types can be made even
larger by disbudding at the proper time. Spoons
and quills are the favorites of many gardeners.
The attractive petals of the former are little tubes
that open at the ends to form tiny spoons, large
enough for a humming bird (if it used spoons).
The quills, their tubes very much twisted or
almost straight add another interesting type to
the collection.

My favorites are the spidery Fujiis, perhaps because they offer a definite challenge in
our area. When I first ordered a collection, I was
told that they would not flower during our late
falls and could not survive our cold winters. Unwilling to give in to our climatic conditions without
a struggle, I looked around for a protected place

for them. The right location was there. To the
east of the storage shed, under the sun deck is a
spot where the chilly winds cannot hit them directly. The sun rides low in the south at this late
time of year shedding its rays on that corner for
a greater part of the day.

In early October I drive long bamboo poles
at the edge of the bed. These are arched and
secured at the top to the sundeck railing. Over
this framework, I stretch a large sheet of trans-
parent plastic, fastening it with clothespins. In
this cozy area the Fujiis start blooming in late
October and the last of them grace our Thanks-
giving table each year. Not only have they survived, but through cuttings made in the spring,
have multiplied so the area is now filled with them.

Chrysanthemums are a pleasure to raise.
They are practically pest-free, their pungent foliage apparently not considered a delicacy in the
insect world. They make wonderful cut flowers
that last for weeks, and are most adaptable for
arrangements. The plants can be moved at almost
any time if it is done carefully. All you need to
do is to water them thoroughly the day before.
(A turgid plant always withstands moving better).
Then prepare the new spot by digging a hole deep
enough to receive the root clump. Drive a spade
straight down being careful not to disturb the
roots. Lift out the clump and place it in its new
location. Water it well with a starter hormone
added to the water, replace the soil, and watch it
grow. It will bloom even after the move.

In one spot I moved three tall chrysanthemum plants from the center of a bed to the outside.
This will leave room for Oriental poppies in the
middle where they can be left undisturbed and
receive a minimum of water during dormancy. The
foliage of the peonies and the mums will give color
and interest after the poppies are gone.

Chrysanthemums can be purchased in pots
late in the season. As they are in bloom at the
time, you can easily select the colors and types

you like. Then you can remove them from the pot and plant them where you wish while the colors are there to guide you.

In spring when the shoots of the chrysanthemums are about six inches long it is time to make cuttings to start new plants. Simply cut off a shoot about four inches long, strip it of all leaves but the tuft at the top, insert the stem in a mixture of equal parts sand and soil, and set it in a sheltered place to root. I use a plant flat for this purpose. I have started as many as three dozen plants in a flat. When they have taken root, they can be moved directly to a flower bed if you have the time to tend them carefully. Because of the amount of work I have to do, I place the rooted cuttings in four inch pots and place them all in one location where I can tend them easily until they are large enough to be placed out in the beds and borders. I am afraid that if I did not do it this way, the mortality rate would be very great.

When you remove the cuttings from the mother plant, be sure to leave one or two sets of leaflets on the old plant. From the base of the two leaflets opposite each other there will appear a new shoot. When this is three or four inches long, pinch off the tip, and it will again branch out. Each time you pinch, you will have another extra stem. You may continue this pinching until the end of June, or mid-July for the late varieties. This will give you bushy, flower covered plants instead of leggy ones.

Chrysanthemum plants should be renewed at least every three years. Old plants tend to become woody and eventually die out. You can make your new ones from cuttings and have a never ending supply to replace the old plants. These and a few new ones purchased now and then should give you a beautiful late garden.

13. THE HERB GARDEN

How many times have you told yourself that you have no place to start an herb garden? Were you thinking of the formal, neatly-landscaped knot garden of colonial days? Or, did you think that the herbs must be grouped together in a special place by the kitchen door?

I'll show you my herbs planted here and there where space allows, where the surroundings are to their liking, and where they are protected from chance mishaps. Rosemary, which was started by an old family friend, has been placed on the edge of the rock walls that build up the flower beds in the lower yard. There the plant drapes over the wall, within easy reach and somewhat protected from the wind by its location. Oregano grows on the raised bed in the vegetable garden and under the large rocks that form the walls of a flower bed. Parsley is everywhere - close to the rocks that form terraces, under the evergreens that form a windbreak on the west, and among the raspberry canes. As this plant is a biennial, a few seed heads left to ripen and drop, insure that we'll have parsley each succeeding year. Old fashioned thyme, lemon thyme (which is more tender) and pineapple thyme are in the raised beds where the fruit trees are planted just inside the gate to the vegetable garden.

Lemon balm, a start of which was given me by a friend grows in most of the perennial beds. It reproduces abundantly and the extra plants are given away regularly. Chives, which must be separated every two or three years, hide under the rosebushes, and mint grows by the water taps where it receives the moisture it needs for abundant growth. Sage drapes over the edge of the phlox bed. Dill, which is an annual, grows here and there in the vegetable garden. As it self-sows very readily, if allowed to go to seed, one need never be without a fresh supply of dill as long as the growing season lasts.

Lavender bushes provide blossoms for sachets. It's fun to use herbs in cooking, and a dash of this or that make a gourmet dish out of a very commonplace recipe.

Herbs are divided into three general groups: perennials, biennials, to which parsley belongs, and annuals. The perennials that include oregano, winter savory, rosemary and the thymes will live for years once they have become established. They may be found in small pots in nurseries during the spring and transplanted to their permanent homes in the garden.

 Dill

 Sweet Basil

 Chives

 Thyme

 Sweet Marjoram

 Rosemary

Marjoram, which is also listed as a perennial, should be planted in a pot and taken indoors or placed in the greenhouse in the winter. It is tender and will not survive our winters. Herbs should be protected during their first winter, and particularly rosemary should have some light shelter. Although I have been very fortunate with mine, many people find it temperamental, and difficult to start and to keep free of winter damage.

A gardening friend gave me an unusual herb called Dittany of Crete which used to live in a pot outdoors during the summer, but must be brought inside during the cold weather. Leaves from a rose geranium that winters in the greenhouse give a delectable flavor to jellies that make attractive Christmas gifts.

Basil, which holds an important place in the cuisine of the Mediterranean countries is an annual. Prepare some good planting soil in a flat, or fruit lug. Plant seed according to directions. Keep the soil moist. A plastic tent will help to retain moisture. When the little plants are one and a half to two inches high, transplant them to their permanent bed, placing them about six inches apart. As soon as they have established themselves, pinch off the tips to encourage branching. It may be well to protect your basil bed with some of that low wire fencing that comes in sections. Surround your basil bed, and lay leafy branches over the top of the area until the plants get used to all-day sun.

Many of you have told me that you tried and liked the sweet basil sauce (pesto) for which I gave you a recipe. Why not plant some basil now?

You might also like to try coriander. Although it may not go to seed, the leaves are interesting and tasteful in salads and fruit cups.

All kitchen herbs mentioned can be dried for use in cooking. Simply cut off the edible parts, wash well and dry in a very slow oven or out in the sunlight. Then crush the leaves

between your palms and store in small glass jars.
You must be sure that both jars and herbs are
dry as moisture will cause them to spoil. Start
with a few herbs and add more to your collection
as you learn about their uses.

PESTO SAUCE

There are probably as many pesto recipes
as there are cooks. The following is the one I
use:
> 3 cups basil leaves
> 1 cup parsley
> 1/2 to 3/4 cup olive oil
> 4 large cloves garlic

Cut garlic into small pieces. Put into
blender with enough oil to cover blades. Blend
until completely mixed with oil.

Add 1/2 of the basil leaves and blend at
low speed. Add rest of oil and basil leaves and
blend again.

Remove to a tightly covered container and
place in refrigerator.

When ready to use on pasta, heat 1/4 cup
of sauce with 2 Tbs. butter or margarine, 2 or 3
Tbs. hot water, and a heaping Tbs. of Parmesan
cheese.

Use on spaghetti or noodles with more
Parmesan cheese. (Don't go near anyone after
eating this delicious dish.) Serves 6-8.

14. THE GARDEN POOL

"The pool 'neath the shade of the old linden tree."

Do you remember that song from the tale of the frog prince who had to live in the pool until the spell cast by the wicked witch was broken? The day of frog princes in ponds is long gone, but a pool as part of your landscaping may be just the thing to lift your garden out of the ordinary. Pools for fish and water vegetation are becoming more and more a part of the garden scene. Large or small, deep or shallow (not less than twelve or fifteen inches to be practical) stationary or movable, you may be able to find a place for one in your yard.

A permanent concrete and stone pool is quite an undertaking, and of course, must be built and placed with great care. Thought should be given to the surroundings, light and shade, draining facilities, ease of cleaning and winter care. If you are going to the trouble and expense to put in a concrete pool, perhaps it will be just as well to make a rather large one that can accommodate fish and other aquatic life as well as a number of plants. A pool two feet deep will take care of the largest hardy lilies available for home pools and the beautiful lotus which must be planted in a round container if it is to live and grow. The lotus must be moved to a frost free spot over the winter.

Water lilies must have sun all day if they are to bloom well. A pool surrounded by tall vegetation that curtails the sunlight, or overhanging trees that keep away the light will result in few or no blossoms. However, the plants will produce an abundance of leaves to cover the surface of the water.

Fish and snails are essential to a clean pool. They eat decayed vegetable matter and the larvae of mosquitoes that lay their eggs on little rafts in the water. The balance of nature is maintained by the fish eating snail eggs so that few are left to hatch and produce an overpopulation in the pool.

My back yard is terraced so that a large pool was easily built at the top level. My nephew dug a hole over two feet deep at the outer edge, and about half that deep at the inner side. It was finished with concrete and large stones according to a set of the many directions one finds in garden magazines, and the instructions and efforts of a very interested old friend of the family. The pool is almost round, a five foot circle almost two feet deep forming the deeper part. The shallow

ground level.

soil

Cement floor and sides

soil level

Drain

Tiny fish can hide among rocks.

Pool is located so this side is above ground level of terraced beds below.

Blocks under flower pots also provide safety areas for fish.

end, only half as deep is shaped like a crescent
eight feet wide.   Water lilies in pots are sunk in
the deeper area, either on the floor of the pool or
on cement blocks to adjust the height according to
the length of the stems of the lilies.   The lotus
is in a half-barrel in the deeper part and it raises
its blooms above the surface of the water.

The deep end of the pool has a large
drain made of a length of two-inch pipe.   When
the plug is removed, the pool is quickly drained
for cleaning of leaves and other things brought in
by the wind.   When the water line drops to less
than half the depth, I place a large tub under the
opening and the fish which come out are caught in
a net and placed in the pool water that has been
caught in the tub.   There they remain until the
pool has been cleaned, refilled, and the water
allowed to settle for a day or two.   This is done
twice a year and is really easy.   The water which
flows out is diverted into several flower beds by
means of a moveable galvanized pipe, so two purposes are served at once.   Firms that sell water
lilies, fish and other pool material advise against
much changing of water in the pool, but I find
this necessary since the birch and the smoke tree
drop debris into the pool.

Again, our cats with the aid of my dog,
Muffie, keep close watch, so they must be thwarted.
A high water level against the steep sides of the
pool together with large white quartz rocks arranged so there are passageways between them are
placed to afford safety for the denizens of the
pool.   Needless to say, the stones are kept totally
submerged since I have seen Dusty balancing himself carefully on a rock that projected above the
water's surface.   Even though cats do not like
water, they are willing to risk a little dampness if
they can take careful aim and swat a fish onto
the grass where it becomes helpless.

Hardy goldfish can be left in the pool during the winter provided it is deep enough and
does not freeze over completely.   The snails

disappear only to return the following spring.
The hardy lilies spend the winter in the pool
below the level of the ice covering.

THE TINY POOL

You looked around in your garden and
found no place for a large pool. Your yard may
be too small and you do not feel that you can give
that much space to it. Maybe you are too busy
with other phases of landscaping at the present
time. Or, the best reason of all, you have young
children, or the pool would be too readily accessible to other neighborhood youngsters.

For you, the little pool may be the answer.
Filled with water plants, it becomes a water garden, and the yen to get into it seems to be less
when there is not a large expanse of water to
tempt little ones.

I have been reading with interest a water
lily catalog and it has given me an idea for something that would not be practical in my large pool
which receives too much shade from the surrounding trees. I hope in the very near future to be
able to buy a night blooming water lily which must
receive sun all day if it is to bloom late in the
evening only to have the blooms close by mid-
morning on the following day.

The catalog suggests many small pools,
most of them movable. They may be galvanized
tubs, discarded baby bathtubs, a barrel cut in
two, or the most versatile of all, a pool made of
black polyethylene film (.006 thickness) which will
last several years and can be mended with asbes-
tos roof cement. The film lined pool can be
shaped any way you wish, the many different
ways limited only by your imagination and amount
of space available.

Although the pools made of various tubs
need not be placed in the ground, it is better to
do so as this greatly reduces the temperature
changes of the water. It should not take long to

Barrel set in sandy base

A sunken tub makes an excellent small pool. Stones and plants around the edge give a permanent feeling.

Outside of barrel treated with wood preservative.

dig a hole for one of these pools. After they are set in, a border of bricks or stones will make it appear very permanent indeed. It is suggested that poolside plants be used for added interest and charm.

Many types of plants can be used in your pool. Some may be planted in two to four inches of soil in pots submerged in an equal amount of water. Others need only one inch of water over them, or may be planted at water level. Some may be planted in pots that are entirely submerged, and will not grow above the surface of the water. Others must be planted in deep water and will rise well above its surface since they will attain heights ranging to six feet. Plants such as water hyacinth and water lettuce float freely on the surface.

Most water plants are very attractive. They are relatively inexpensive, so if storage is a problem, replacement will not prove a hardship. However, this does not apply to the lilies which

are more costly, but are worth the effort it takes
to find a wintering-over place for the ones that
are not hardy. They may be placed in clay pots
or other types of containers since, in their case,
drainage is no problem. Containers made from
clean plastic bleach, detergent, water softener and
anti-freeze containers of various shapes and sizes
will fit into many spots in your pool or pools.

My catalog also suggests wooden boxes as
containers, but discourages the use of redwood as
it will discolor the water. Containers can be ele-
vated to the right height by placing them on
bricks or cement blocks. It also stresses the fact
that at least an inch of sand be placed on the
bottom of the plastic pool to lessen the possibility
of damage to the material by placing a container
upon it.

Miniature water lilies called pygmae lilies
may be used in tub gardens or pools. They will
grow with four inches of water above them, but
will be happier with eight inches. Some water iris

A raised pool may be made by
using flat stones cemented together for the sides and built on
a three-inch cement base.
Line pool with polyethelene film.
Cover base with sand so pots won't
damage film.

ranging from one to two feet in height may be planted in your pool.

Algae forms when sunlight strikes a pool, but water lilies need light in order to bloom. Plants with leaves that cover the surface of the water help cut down on the algae. So do snails which eat it, as they do the decaying vegetation and excess fish food in the pool. Goldfish do wonders in keeping down the mosquito population, and the water plants supply oxygen and hiding places for the tiny fish.

Hardy goldfish will live over in an outdoor pool in the winter. For their well-being, it is suggested that they be in a submerged pool in which the change in water temperature is not so drastic. An opening in the ice should be provided so gases trapped under it can escape. Otherwise, the fish may be taken out in late fall and placed in a tub in the greenhouse or a well-lighted garage. A securely fastened screen should be placed over the container. Our cats went fishing in the uncovered tub in the greenhouse several winters ago with the result that new fish had to be purchased.

The catalog also stresses pools with steep sides so that plants can be placed close to the edges as the shade they produce will help with the algae problem.

The beauty of these small pools is that they can be bailed dry and moved to another spot if you find the first location to be unsatisfactory. It takes a very short time to assemble one. However, a container full of water does not make a pool or water garden. Get a catalog, study it carefully and plan what you want in your pool. Then order your plant material and prepare your containers so you can get right to work when they arrive.

15. BE KIND TO OUR FEATHERED FRIENDS

Happiness is a humming bird that finds itself in a great wide world of almost an acre and a half which must have been made just for him. At least that must have been the first thought of the tiny bird that came to our premises several years ago and has returned ever since with his mate. For a time he was joined by another couple, but for the last two or three years they have not returned.

So many of us say that we have planted this or that because the birds love it. We do plant berry bushes such as those that produce an abundance of holly berries, pyracantha berries, snowberries, and some things that we do not share so willingly such as cherries, raspberries and strawberries. We plant an abundance of bachelor buttons which make the little canaries happy, and poppy seeds are picked up by other birds. There is no telling how many weeds never see the light of day because our feathered friends found the seeds before they could ripen.

Then one day we are surprised by a little humming bird flitting in and out among the plants in the flower beds. He is going at the monarda with great gusto. Next he darts up to a tall campanula and sinks his beak deep into its throat. A clump of day lilies attracts his attention next.

Suddenly he is gone. A few minutes later he is over in the neighbor's yard doing an animated aerial dance around the hollyhocks. From these he flies to the Rose of Sharon bushes and visits their inviting blooms. Whether or not he takes nectar from these, I do not know. But he is attracted to them and flies from one bush to the other for some time.

Across the street another garden has

spread an attractive banquet for him. Tall red hot
pokers with their hundreds of tube-like flowers rise
above the petunias, both offering many deep cups
from which he can sip the nectar upon which he
feeds. Near by is a blue mist spirea just beginning to burst into bloom. It too, has deep-throated
blooms and offers a new source of food when the
pokers have finally run their course.

It's time to fly across the street again.
He's flying around the petunias on the sun deck
now. Here one of his favorite spots for food
abounds until the last days of fall. A very much
belated wisteria has just decided to bloom. The
long cluster of blossoms catches his eye and in
an instant that long bill is deep in the throat of
one of the flowers.

The silk tree is another of his favorites.
The pink tassels have a delightful odor and each

morning and evening he visits them.

When planning the garden for next year, put some plants there for the hummers. All those mentioned above are found in large numbers in our three garden areas. Then there is the physostegia with its tall spikes of orchid-pink just beginning to bloom. The trumpet vine that is now climbing the nite-guard pole has many clusters of deep-throated, red-orange flowers to tempt humming birds. I have even seen one hovering near the huge hibiscus blooms. They are attracted to bright colors. One of my friends told me that they fly close to her when she wears a certain bright print as she works in the garden.

Make a little bit of heaven for a tiny bird. He will more than repay you by his frequent visits to your home. He may even bring his mate along and make a home on the branch of a tree or shrub.

SEED CAKES CAN STOP THOSE BIRD-FEED WOES

Birdseed cakes solved a long-standing problem for me. I have two windows - one the south-facing living room window and another at an angle to it, that are not accessible to cats. For this reason they are an excellent spot for feeding birds in winter. However, they are above a flower bed and bird seed placed in trays on these two windows landed in the flower beds as much or more than it did in the birds' stomachs.

In the spring, grass came up in the flower bed and had to be pulled out before a young lawn threatened to overrun the bed. The thought of seed cakes as an answer to feeding birds, eliminating the waste of seed and preventing the start of unwanted patches of grass came to me as a solution to the problem.

I make seed cakes from a combination of beef suet which I buy at a butcher shop, and chicken and bacon fats which I save from my cooking. Most of the fat is from the suet which is firm and melts at a higher temperature than either of the other two. Three parts of suet to one part of either or a combination of the other fats makes a good foundation for the seed cake. (The butcher will be glad to run the suet through the grinder so as to make it easier to render).

Put two or three quarts of water into a large saucepan and place the fat in it. Bring the contents to a boil and turn the heat down so that they will simmer for an hour or more. Remove the saucepan from the stove and set it in a cool place so that the fats will congeal. (The fats should be boiled in water as this will remove salt and other chemicals. Simply rendering the fats without water will not remove elements that may be harmful to the birds.) Skim the fat from the saucepan and place it in a container in which it may be stored until needed.

Place a small amount of fat - the amount that will melt to a half-inch in depth - in a loaf tin. Add seed to the melted fat and stir well until each seed is coated. Keep adding seeds as long as there is enough fat to coat them. You will be surprised at the amount of seed that will be coated. Smooth the surface of the cakes and place them in the freezer until such time as you wish to use them.

Remove the seed cake from the pan by dipping it into very hot water. Put each cake on a styrofoam tray and place it where the birds can get it, but cats cannot. It is surprising to find how long a seed cake will last. Each seed must be picked out individually. There is no loss because of spilling or scratching them out of the container.

Wrap extra seed cakes in foil and store them in the freezer until needed. And what about making a few seed cakes to give to your friends for their bird feeders? They make an excellent gift for oldsters who would find it hard to make their own.

16. SPRING FLOWERING BULBS

The early bulbs are my favorites, because I start getting garden fever in February and it is at this time that they begin venturing out. Snow may still be on the ground when the first snow-drops push up through the soil under the rose-bushes to announce that spring is on the way.

Snowdrops should be planted six inches deep in light soils and four inches deep in heavier soils. They should be planted closely together in a spot that will be shady as soon as your shrubs or trees leaf out.

Squills and scillas are of many kinds. Most of them are blue, but you may find a purple-pink and a white variety. They average six inches in height and bloom very early. The blue ones are startling in their clear colors and make a fine combination with white and yellow crocuses.

Wood hyacinths come in dark blue, light blue, white and rose pink. They are taller than those mentioned in the preceding paragraph, and the blooms cover much of the upper part of the erect spikes.

Glory-of-the-snow come in a startling, beautiful blue, rosy pink, or white. They too like a place close to shrubbery, under trees, or in banks where they won't be disturbed. Most of mine are planted under a stone retaining wall, and when in bloom, catch everyone's eyes.

The grape hyacinth come in white and blue and are familiar to everyone. These charm-ing border plants multiply rapidly and in a short time the new bulbs can be tucked here and there among the spaces in the rock garden, by the pool, and under the evergreens.

Winter aconite blooms in February and March in shady spots. The flowers are yellow and resemble buttercups, but most of them are much larger. They like moisture, so when planting them, be sure they are readily accessible for watering.

Dog-tooth-violet, despite its ugly common name, is among the loveliest of spring bulbs. The flowers look like a small yellow lily, borne several to a stem, and the variegated foliage is very attractive. These bulbs may be left undisturbed for many years in a somewhat shaded area that provides moist but well-drained soil.

Perhaps the crocuses should be mentioned in this group, even though they are familiar to everyone. They may be had in the traditional yellow, and in lavender, white and variegated purple. Planted in drifts around the bases of trees and in the border, they come back year after year. They multiply rapidly and in a few years a few dozen bulbs number hundreds.

Brodiaea prevers a sunny location by a south wall or in the rock garden. The bulbs should be planted four inches apart and divided every fourth year. They should be heavily mulched in late fall.

You are perhaps wondering why I have not told you at what depth most of these bulbs should be planted. Usually, a bulb is happiest planted at a depth of three times the height of the bulb. If the soil is light and sandy, they may be placed an inch or so deeper. If the soil is heavy, I advise mixing it with sand and soil conditioner because the flowers will otherwise have a hard time pushing to the surface any may be malformed.

All bulbs, whether they are partial to moisture or not, still want good drainage, so be sure that the area drains well. They should also be fed, and the best time for this is planting time.

A trench should be dug where the bulbs are to be placed. The soil should be loosened at least four inches deeper than the depth at which the bulb is to be planted. Sand and grit should be added to the soil if necessary along with soil conditioner.

The soil at the bottom of the trench is mixed generously with bone meal or superphosphate (0-20-0) and a covering of one inch of soil placed over it. The bulbs are them placed on the soil and covered. They are then watered, covered with the steer manure, and left to wait until spring.

Usually we get enough moisture during the winter to care for them. If we have a very dry year, I take advantage of a warm day to water the spots where they are planted as I water other areas dried out by the sun and wind.

I try to get these bulbs in the ground no later than late September. Tulips, narcissus, and hyacinths can be planted as late as October or November, but these little ones that are not planted so deeply must have time to produce roots before the earth freezes too hard.

MORE ABOUT BULBS

Have you ever seen a strangely beautiful new flower and found that it comes from a bulb that can be raised in your garden? Such an experience happened to me when I saw a Fritillaria imperialis in a local nursery. The stalk of this interesting plant will grow to three feet in height. At the top is an upright tuft of shiny green leaves. Under this crest, pendant blossoms of yellow, orange, or red-orange form a large cluster that brightens the garden in early May. This facinating plant has two oddities. First and most important, the bulb, which must be planted at a depth of six to eight inches, should be laid on its side. This is to prevent it from rotting if water gets into it after the stalk has fallen away. The second is that the plant has a powerful odor resembling that of a skunk. However, since it is outdoors and need not be too close to the house, that is a small matter. Six of these beauties in my garden do not bother anyone with their odor. These flowers are said to keep away those rodents that skunks battle, since the odor leads them to think one of their enemies is near.

Another member of this family is the guinea hen flower. It is only six inches tall, and the pendant bells are somewhat angular in shape and checkered in various colors. This little bulb is planted four inches deep in shady spots. It likes rich, moist loam to which some sharp sand has been added.

Long ago a nice lady in Sparks gave me several colchicum bulbs. They are fascinating plants. The bulbs, which are poisonous, should be planted three to four inches deep in rich soil around the bases of shrubs, near rocks, or other spots where they will not be disturbed. Colchicums are ideal for those people who can't wait, but must have their blooms now. The nurseries will have these in by the latter part of July. They should be planted immediately, and in September the lilac and pinkish blooms will appear out of the ground as if by magic. After two or three weeks they will fade away and disappear. Early in the spring a huge cluster of leaves that resemble those of the skunk cabbage will push their way out of the ground. They should not be cut off, but left to mature and wither away. In July, a gentle tug will pull the leaves away from the bulbs that will then lie dormant until September again calls them to show their colors. Several clumps of colchicums of many shades hide in various corners in my garden. If by chance I uproot a bulb as I pull at the foliage I plant it elsewhere and start a new clump. They multiply well, and soon a few will produce enough for other locations.

One could write pages on alliums. These decorative members of the onion family come in many sizes and colors. Tallest is Allium giganteum, which grows to four feet and produces a beautiful purple head the size of an indoor baseball. Not quite so tall, but very striking, is Allium albopilosum which grows to two feet. It produces a huge ball of light purple flowers that fade away, but leave spikes on their stalk and make attractive dried arrangements. The tiny yellow

Allium moly naturalizes well, spreads rapidly, and is excellent for cutting. Allium karataviense produces three broad, flat leaves of mottled green and purple. The round bloom is larger than a tennis ball and nestles in the leaf cluster so the plant is not much more than six inches tall. It is very effective in a rock garden or close to a wall.

There are several other alliums available for your garden. All these plants like rich loam, good drainage, and should be planted to three times the bulb height in the soil. Bone meal or superphosphate (0-20-0) placed under them, as explained in the preceding chapter, will furnish food for better plants. They multiply readily and should be divided every three or four years.

Anemones, camassias, hardy cyclamen, and ranunculus provide interest in the spring garden. Anemone tubers should be kept dry until planting time. They should then be soaked in water for forty-eight hours before planting. If planted in fall, they must be given winter protection. Spring plantings can be made after the soil is warm. Hardy cyclamen likes a home under a tall shrub or dwarf tree where it gets partial shade and moisture. Camassias and ranunculus are happy in the sunshine, but must be given winter protection and watered well. However, they do want good drainage.

Be sure your soil is well prepared before planting these bulbs. They will remain in a certain spot for a long while, and good soil preparation will insure beautiful blooms for a long time. Remember the bone meal or superphosphate (0-20-0) at planting time, and a top dressing of manure in very early spring.

Foliage from our spring blooming bulbs will be pretty unsightly in a little while. Try not to see it, and leave it to produce food to feed the bulbs. Although it is recommended that bulbs be left alone during the dormant period into late summer you may have to move them earlier for

some reason. Moving them to another home may
be accomplished by lifting the whole bulb mass
without disturbing the soil and placing the clump
into a box where you will leave it until planting
time in the fall. As soon as the foliage has died
down, place the box in a cool corner and leave
it alone until planting time. Or you may wish
to move a clump to another spot before you forget where the empty space is. Dig a hole in
the new location, lift up the entire clump and
cover with soil to its original depth. It will
never know that it was moved if you are careful
not to disturb the roots. Otherwise you may
lose the bulbs.

Some time ago, I was at a gathering where
the subject came around to bulbs and problems
with squirrels and chipmunks. They do love to
dig down and eat the bulbs. I suggested a solution that has worked well with many who have
been plagued with the problem. Chicken wire –
the kind with small holes – works well in cases
like this. Plant bulbs in clumps or in rows by
digging out the soil, being sure to dig far enough
down so that a sprinkling of superphosphate
(0-20-0) can be added to the subsoil. Cover the
fertilizer an inch or so with soil, plant the bulbs,
add some more soil and top this with a sheet of
chicken wire long enough and wide enough so that
it can be tucked under about three inches all
around. Then fill the planted area to the proper
depth with soil and water it down well. The wire
should remain in the bed until time to dig the bed
up again to renew it. Somewhere I have read that
sprinkling moth crystals an inch or so below the
surface of the soil will discourage varmints that
will be repelled by the odor. The buried crystals
will last much longer than if they were sprinkled
on top and exposed to the air.

Laying the chicken wire on top of the
planting is effective is one does not mind the
appearance and is going to dig up the bulbs when
the blooms are gone. However one must be sure

the edges are securely fastened so that pests cannot tunnel underneath it.

Mulch after the first heavy frost that has frozen the top layer of soil. To do so before that only invites pests to dig into the soft earth and get into the plantings. Although I live on the outskirts of town and chipmunks and squirrels abound here, I have no trouble with my bulb plantings. The best way to foil squirrels and mice? Two very busy and active cats!

17. TENDER PLANTS NEED WINTER PROTECTION

It seems strange that one must think of moving plants back into the house and greenhouse during the hot days of early fall. However, that annual hard freeze that comes suddenly during the early part of September has made those of us who have indoor gardens wary.

Houseplants and those that are hardy enough to spend the winter in a cold greenhouse must be prepared for that move, which involves several steps. First of all, check all those plants which are in pots. If roots are coming out of the drainhole at the bottom, it is time to move the plant to a larger container. Note all changes to be made and arrange for enough pots of the right size. If the pots are old, scrub them with soapy water and a brush. I no longer sterilize them by placing them in the oven and turning on the heat as it takes so much time. Now I soak them in a chlorine solution instead.

Soil mixtures are made according to the needs of the plants to be repotted. The plants are watered the day before the repotting takes place. It is then easy to place the root ball on the bed of soil in the larger pot and fill in around the edges with fresh soil. There will be more pots to scrub and sterilize when this is over.

The greenhouse is next on the list. All plants that have summered there are moved out under nearby trees. Any little frogs found hiding among the flower pots are caught and put outdoors among the ground covers. Then a strong solution of Clorox is sprayed over the entire inside surface of the greenhouse. I make sure the benches and walls are drenched. In a few days everything is dry and the odor has disappeared.

All plants that can be sprayed with either

malathion or diazinon are given a good spraying the day after they have been watered. Then, although I do not use systemics outdoors, I give each plant a dose of a systemic designated for houseplants according to its size. This will remove white flies, other chewing insects, and their young which might hatch within the next few weeks.

The plants that spent the summer outdoors are returned to their winter quarters, friends who are waiting for slips receive them, and I am left with the task of placing the remaining plants in the best spot for them.

The more tender plants that do not need a great deal of sun are placed on greenhouse shelves close to the wall of the house. The fuchsias, which by now have trailed down below the hanging pots, are cut off to about eight inches and hung on hooks close to the glass panes. Begonia feasti can survive there in winter, so the extra ones are placed close to the wall. The pluroma, which is now blooming in ernest, takes its place behind the door by mid-September. The shrimp plants go indoors in late September, while the tuberous begonias remain outside until a hard frost kills the stems and leaves.

Many times I leave some plants outside until the end of September or even later because I have a sheltered corner for them. If an unusually cold night threatens, I drive bamboo stakes into the ground around them and drape them with a plastic covering, which must be removed early in the morning before the sun's rays get too warm.

Cuttings made from geraniums are allowed to callus for a few hours and then placed in a mixture of sand and soil. The container is placed in the greenhouse so it will get sun only part of the day during the first month or so, and then is moved to a sunnier spot in the greenhouse after the new plants have begun to root.

Pelargoniums and the one-of-a-kind geraniums, which I keep in pots, must be moved into the greenhouse early in September because they are subject to frost bite. Coleus plants are too tender to survive there through the winter, so I make a small cutting of each of my favorites and keep them in the house during the winter. Those that are planted in the ground are left there for Jack Frost, along with the extra genaniums that have been blooming in one of the flower beds.

When the begonias have finally died down, I gently remove the stems and move the pots into the greenhouse. Since the tubers are very close to the top of the soil, I fill in the tops of the pots with ground bark until it is even with the rims. The pots are then stacked in a corner. Later in fall I cover them with plastic to keep the tubers from drying out.

The greenhouse windows and door stay open until the night temperatures drop to near freezing. Then they are closed at night, but remain open on pleasant days. When day temperatures drop into the fifties, the door and windows stay closed, and by late November a sheet of clear plastic covers all the glass and provides a two-inch dead air space as insulation throughout the winter. Over the years I have found that a plant which can survive San Francisco's winter outdoors is safe in the cold greenhouse during our winter.

If warm weather persists into very late fall, another feeding of systemic is used to prevent any insects from attacking the plants before the windows are closed. There is a liquid (0-10-10) fertilizer fortified with yucca extract on the market. It is supposed to make plants more winter-hardy, as it strengthens the roots but does not promote top growth. I'm going to try it in the greenhouse. I have used it on several rather delicate outdoor shrubs, and they came through the winter very well. Whatever you do, DON'T feed plants with a nitrogen fertilizer after mid-July. New growth, which would be evident some six weeks after that date, will be very tender and fall prey to an early frost.

Inside greenhouse facing
west. Storage space under shelf
to the south is below ground level.
Glass panes to the west are stationary,
while those to the south may be opened.

18. TUBEROUS BEGONIAS GO TO SLEEP

Those of you who plant your tuberous begonias in pots may be interested in this manner of storing the tubers through the winter. I've planted these beauties for years and at one time followed directions as to winter storage religiously. I removed them from the pots, removed the excess soil from around the tubers and stored them as directed. Then I went through the regular routine of planting them for the following season.

At that time I lived in a house that had a glassed-in, but unheated back porch. Several of the begonias sat on a desk by the east wall where the sun shone most of the day. The rest of the pots were clustered with other plants in a small bed by the back door during the summer months.

One winter I forgot to remove one of the pots from the back porch and it stayed there all winter. Our old tomcat decided that he liked the big pot and spent a great deal of his time curled up in it. Spring came and I removed the pot and was very much surprised to see small buds pushing up through the soil. They were just as healthy as those that had been painstakingly stored in the basement. That was more than twenty-five years ago, and I have never dug up the tubers for winter storage since that time.

Now I have an unheated greenhouse in much the same situation as that back porch of long ago. Anything that will live outdoors in winter in the bay area, is safe there in winter. I bring the plants into the greenhouse after having removed the withered leaves and stems. Each pot is filled to the brim with finely ground bark. The pots are then stacked three deep under one of the benches, the top pot in each group mounded high with more of the bark and the entire group covered with a large sheet of plastic.

Late in March I remove the covering, and give each pot a cupful of water, and cover them again. Late in April this is repeated once more, and finally May comes and it is time to repot the tubers. I prepare a mix of leaf mold and commercial potting soil in equal parts. Then I take out the pots, dump the protecting bark from the top and lift the tubers carefully since most have tiny shoots at this time. I lay these carefully in a tray, dump the old soil and rinse the pots in a solution of chlorine and water. The pots are then rinsed, and filled to within an inch of the rim with the new soil mix. Tubers should be placed so that they are barely covered with about an inch of soil and then watered and set in a warm place to start growth.

Late in May the danger of frost is usually gone, but it is a good idea to place the pots outside under low growing shrubs or among taller plants that will give them some protection. If a cold night threatens, it is easy to drape a protecting sheet over the shrub or the taller plants to keep the frost from harming the tender young plants hiding among them.

In June the pots may be moved to their summer homes in dappled shade. The regular weekly feedings of half strength fish emulsion should begin now and continue until the last blooms are gone.

PROVES A TEST FOR HARDINESS

A number of my readers have expressed interest in a cold greenhouse, but have wondered if it would be worth their while. Perhaps this chapter may help them make a decision.

Our long, cold spell during the winter of 1970-71 made a testing area of mine. The relative hardiness of certain plants was proved, and I shall be better able to decide where to winter certain tender plants. The greenhouse was built for those plants that require a period of dormancy and cannot stand our cold winters outside in the garden. It also takes care of those reasonably hardy plants that are not too happy in a dry, warm indoor situation. In the greenhouse they undergo a period of relative inactivity, but are only semi-dormant and are ready to start growth as soon as a few warm days raise the temperature 10 degrees or so.

Only once has water frozen to a thickness of almost a quarter of an inch in a bucket which I keep in the greenhouse to help me gauge the temperature. However, nothing happened to any of the plants during those few days, the water did not freeze again, and all went well.

After reviewing the situation in mid-March, I can make the following observations. The cold, which for the first time defoliated the fuchsias, did not harm the pelargoniums or the other two geraniums which each had a bloom at the time. A beefsteak begonia which I left in the greenhouse until too late to bring indoors did the unexpected. It came through the cold weather with a few leaves frozen on the side that was away from the wall of the house, and shortly sent forth new leaves. A purple-leafed zebrina weathered the winter on a table where it received a maximum of winter sunlight with only minor damage and soon started showing new growth. All the fuchsias which I pruned in late February and early March leafed out and one of them bloomed very soon. Cuttings made from the fuchsias which friends brought me late in the summer from California, did not know that they were not supposed to take root in the fall, and were ready to be removed from the aquarium which was their nursery during the winter. They were placed in pots and set buds very soon after.

I mustn't forget the princess plant. Both the mother plant and a small one made from a cutting did very well. Beside them, a Dittany of Crete listed as a tender herb was shooting out

long tendrils and tiny new leaves were showing.
Also, the group of water lily bulbs that had been
given me last spring were leafing out and remind-
ing me that I had better get busy with that new
sunlit pool I had planned to finish before another
summer went by.

The previous fall I had found a foolish
little leaf clump that was trying to uncurl just as
the first bitterly cold days threatened. I couldn't
identify it at the time, but I knew that it would
never make it through the winter. I placed it in
a pot in a corner of the greenhouse. During
the late winter I watered it once or twice. Shortly, it was boasting four beautiful calla lily leaves
and promising to bloom some time in the spring.

Now, let's go down to No. 4. That is
the name of a well-insulated, well-lighted, but
unheated, cement-floored storage room. It got its
name from its second-hand door with the number
- 4 - on it. There is a sand-bottomed, ventilated,
two foot deep pit at one end of it. There potatoes, onions, garlic, squash, gladious corms and
dahlia tubers spend the winter happily in cool,
dark comfort. But the plants in the room told a
somewhat different story. All the pretty new
geranium plants that had been started decided
that it was too cold there for them. The heavier
rooted old fuchsias lived, but they were leafing
out very slowly. Two tender new ones found the
cold too much for them. Two abutilons kept their
leaves all winter and after a pruning administer-
ed a few weeks before, were showing new growth.

And the best surprise of all came with
the spring. Did you ever hang on to a plant
that didn't bloom for twelve long years? I have
one such which I had bought from a nursery in
Oregon. I was assured that it would take our
winters. It did, twelve of them, but until two
years before, it had died down to the ground each
winter. Each year the beautiful crown of leaves
that sprang from the new branches of the Hydrangea macrophylla caused me to spare its life. Then,

one day I read an article that said that the plant produced blooms on year-old wood. The huge container in which a holly had been brought to my garden became home for the hydrangea. In the fall, the plant with the year's stalks on it was placed in No. 4. Evidently the temperature was right for it, because it leafed out and three tiny, but promising clusters of buds were on its leafy canes.

I hope this chapter will give you an idea of the relative hardiness of some plants which you may wish to own and help you decide if the pleasures of a cold greenhouse are worth the expense and effort.

P.S. This chapter is a record of what happened in the cold greenhouse in a colder than average winter. A very severe winter will cause a great deal of damage.

19. RAPPACCINI'S GARDEN

Nathaniel Hawthorne told a story about an Italian scientist who developed a garden of plants so poisonous that the very air in that beautiful Eden wreaked of toxic vapors. The scientist had his own misguided reasons for nurturing such a deadly retreat.

Our own gardens, though not planned with any ulterior purpose in mind, also abound with plants which are more or less deadly. Often, as I look around at these innocent-looking Borgias of the plant world, I wonder how I ever managed to escape an early death. As a youngster, I was never without a stem of a plant, a leaf, or a shoot of some kind in my mouth. It was my good fortune to have lived out in the country where people had little time and space for flowers and the only plants coaxed along were those in vegetable gardens.

Let's take a walk in the garden to see how many poisonous plants we can find. By the driveway is a huge rhubarb plant. This has long been regarded as an excellent spring tonic as well as a source of delectable sauce and rhubarb pie. Although the stalks are edible and delicious, the leaves contain a poison which can cause convulsions and death.

The larkspur which pops up here and there among the plants in the perennial bed, has poisonous seeds and eating the plant itself may prove fatal. The leaves of foxglove, which are a source of digitalis, and the foliage and roots of bleeding heart and Dutchman's breeches have proved fatal to cattle.

Most early spring bulbs are poisonous, so to be safe, children should be taught while still very young, not to put them into their mouths.

Leaves and flowers of lily-of-the-valley and the bulbs of colchicums are poisonous.

Ornamental shrubs and trees contribute their share toward a modern version of Rappaccini's garden. Berries of daphne and jasmine, seeds and pods of wisteria, and all parts of laurel, rhododendrons and azaleas are poisonous. Most insidious is the yew, because the foliage is even more deadly than the berries, and death comes without any warning symptoms.

Did you know that the twigs and foliage of wild and cultivated cherries contain a compound that releases cyanide when eaten? Don't try it to see if it is true. Less toxic, but also to be avoided, are parts of oak, elderberry and black locust.

Many weeds have poisonous properties. Most members of the nightshade family are poisonous. Some of these are sprawling weeds that bear a white blossom and a green berry which turns whitish and then yellow as it ripens. It resembles a very tiny tomato in shape and is abundantly produced. By the way, did you know that potatoes, peppers, tomatoes and eggplant are members of the nightshade family? Or that belladonna, which is used for its medicinal properties, comes from a member of that group?

Over by the front gate, I had two large datura plants. These are commonly known as angels' trumpets and are as poisonous as their relatives with the lowly name of jimsonweed. After reading in an issue of *Readers' Digest* of the very poisonous properties of this entire plant, I have destroyed them. No longer do the beautiful white trumpets bloom to perfume the air, but none from my garden will summon any little angels home.

In our dry climate we do not find jack-in-the-pulpit, moonseed, or mayapple except perhaps in heavily wooded areas. Jack-in-the-pulpit contains needle-like crystals that will cause intense irritation to membranes of the mouth and tongue. Moonseed berries which resemble small, blue-purple grapes are poisonous. Mayapple plants contain several poisonous ingredients and the fruit can cause severe gastric disturbances.

The oleander that borders highways in parts of California and Arizona is extremely poisonous. You may remember that the villainous owner of Dragonwyck used this plant to free himself of his unwanted wife. Much as I like the appearance of this plant, it is not among my houseplants or those in the greenhouse. (It will not tolerate our winters outdoors.)

Let's go in and take a look at the houseplants. The poinsettias that bloom so beautifully during the holidays are dangerous. Mistletoe berries have caused death, and a single rosary pea seed has been known to be fatal.

Last but not least among the houseplants is the showy dieffenbachia. This plant can choke one to death. Chewing on its leaves and stems releases tiny needle-like crystals that cause intense burning and irritation. Swelling of the tongue areas can block off the air passages and impede breathing.

No list of poisonous plants should omit the exotic-looking castor bean. This gorgeous, ornamental annual with huge leaves and brilliant cluster of blooms at the ends of the branches is very poisonous. Particularly so are the beans that appear in little cases after the blooms have matured. According to my source of information, as few as two have been known to cause death. Usually I have a few of these plants in my garden. However, as soon as a seed pod appears, it is quickly snipped off and relegated to the garbage can. With no children around and a word to all garden visitors, I do not worry about anyone tearing off one of the huge leaves and consuming it.

I hope you will remember this chapter. It does not cover all poisonous plants, but does mention most of those found in our area. Too many people have become very ill or died because someone didn't know the toxic properties of some of his horticultural specimens.

20. BEFORE THE SNOW FLIES

Winter is just around the corner, but we are having some great weather in which to prepare for it. Those who have been here for years know about our unpredictable spring weather and that it is better to put our faith in the long Indian summer to do many jobs. Although some might be delayed until spring, the wise gardener will not do so. Then, of course, there are those that should be done now, not delayed until later.

As usual, one must think ahead to the next growing season. Are changes to be made? New beds? New additions such as raised beds, trellises and so forth?

Once before I recommended "major surgery" to be done in fall and received many favorable comments on the idea. Removal of unwanted trees, shrubs and other growth is easily done now when the soil is still workable and the least damage will be done to surrounding plants as most have gone dormant for the season. This will also give the gardener time to remove the evidence of his activity. It's surprising how much easier it will be to work the newly usable spots once spring comes. New, raised beds are better made now and filled with new earth and additives that will give bacteria a longer time in which to do their work. New beds at ground level? Make them now by removing whatever was in the intended spots and work in the new soil at this time.

Fallen leaves should be raked and removed. Diseased leaves and other debris should be removed and burned or placed in the refuse can to be carted away. Do not place them in flower beds where they will do damage. In renewing old beds, remove the old soil and replace it with new. Weeds can be eradicated easily at this time, and debris that can house pests during the winter should be removed from the premises.

Tools can be given the care they need before they are stored for the winter. Drain, roll up and put away all hoses that will not be used again until next season. Repair all damaged equipment; remove rust from metal parts and coat with a film of furnace oil or stove oil, and put everything away in a protected place.

However, with some plants, success dictates that we make haste slowly. Among the tasks not to be hurried are the harvesting of summer-flowering corms and fleshy rooted plants. The galdioli are gone now, but some of the stalks and leaves still show a considerable amount of green. If you can wait for them to dry completely, by all means do so. If not dig up the corms being careful to leave the stalks attached. Lay them on several thicknesses of newspaper or a sheet of cardboard on the floor of the garage or some other available storage area. Throw a shovelful or so of moist earth on them and wait until the stalk comes off with a gentle tug. Cover the corms with an old blanket if the weather turns unduly cold. When the stalks are removed, dust the corms with powdered sulphur or a good fungicide and put them in a cool, dry place until next spring.

Tuberous begonia foliage seems to hang on and on even though the blooms have gone. This foliage too, must mature before being removed. You should have started withholding water from these plants some time ago. However, if you did not, remove them to a frost-free place and do so now. Allow the tops to die down and then remove them gently from the tubers. The most satisfactory method of winter storage I have found is to place enough peat moss on the top of each pot to come to the top of the rim. Then I stack the pots four or five deep and cover them with an old blanket. Mine are stored in the cold greenhouse. Perhaps you have one, too. Or you could store them in a corner of the garage if it does not freeze there. Get them off the cold floor, throw an old blanket on top of the pots and if the temperature does not fluctuate too much, they will come out of hibernation ready to go in the spring. But, please, please, don't follow the instructions of that "expert" who told my friend to give them a nitrogen feeding before putting them away. They want to sleep, not to eat! Incidentally, out of almost thirty tubers, I have lost about four during the last two or three years. No room for complaint there.

Late in March I remove the covering, and give each pot a cupful of water, and cover them again. Late in April this is repeated once more, and finally May comes and it is time to repot the tubers. I prepare a mix of leaf mold and commercial potting soil in equal parts. Then I take out the pots, dump the protecting bark from the top and lift the tubers carefully since most have tiny shoots at this time. I lay these carefully in a tray, dump the old soil and rinse the pots in a solution of chlorine and water.

I hope you haven't pulled up your dahlias and cannas yet. Like potatoes and onions in the vegetable garden, the roots must have time to mature thoroughly before being dug. One of the foremost causes of loss of these fleshy rooted plants is digging them up before they have fully matured.

When the first frost blackens the leaves and stalks, just leave them until they no longer have any life left in them. Cut them off about two inches above the ground and leave the roots in the ground for another two or three weeks. Then lift them out of the ground carefully leaving as much dirt as possible on the roots. Again, back to that sheltered area for a few days. Inspect the tubers carefully and remove any that do not look healthy. Do not separate them at this time. Dust any cut surfaces with sulphur or a good fungicide. I'm lucky enough to have a small root cellar in No. 4 (our storage area) and there, buried in a fruit lug full of sand, they winter satisfactorily. In the spring when planting time comes, make your divisions of these plants. Be sure that each tuber has a part of the mother stalk attached so it will bloom.

Cut your bamboo or reed canes after the leaves have yellowed or show signs of drying. Lay the canes flat in an out of the way area. They will dry and the leaves can be easily removed in spring when you are ready to use the canes. Or, if you are an orderly soul, you may do it now.

It will soon be time to plant the tulips and hyacinth bulbs. Since it is better to postpone the planting of these until late October or early November, just dig up the area now leaving the holes ready to receive the bulbs at the proper time. I do something which I feel helps to revitalize the soil. The sun is such a powerful factor in sterilizing and renewing the earth that I dig holes for rosebushes as well as bulbs in the fall. These, and the piles of refill earth that is to be used, are left exposed to the sun and air until I am ready for planting. The plants are then set out and covered with the sun-bathed soil. I believe that this practice is responsible for my healthy plantings.

Another word especially for the new gardeners. Your garden still needs water. Even in late fall some deep watering is in order to keep plants from suffering. There is not much evaporation now so the waterings can be spaced farther apart - just don't forget them. Have you noticed how much longer well-watered shrubs and trees retain their colorful leaves? This leads to another point. Don't be in too great a hurry to put the hoses away for the winter. In fact, it's a good idea to leave one out for those occasional winter waterings. A rubber hose is much more suited for this purpose than a plastic hose as the latter become very stiff and brittle in cold weather.

Now let's take a look at the commercial

substances used during the gardening season;
half empty bottles or boxes of fertilizers, herbi-
cides, pesticides - in powder, granule, pellet and
liquid forms. Concentrate all these things in one
or more packages and discard the empty containers in the garbage can, or as suggested by the
manufacturer. Substances, the shelf life of
which has expired, should be thrown out.
They'll only get older the longer they stay
around. Substances that have been banned
for home use should also be disposed of safely.
        Now it's time to assemble all things and
group them according to their kind. Put all fertilizers together, and all pesticides in a safe
place. It will be so much easier to get to them
next year. Remember too, that these substances
are sometimes altered by extreme heat and cold,
so place them if possible in a dark, cool place
with controlled temperature.
        You'll be so proud of yourself when
you've done all these things and you'll look for-
ward to spring with a feeling of things well done.

WINTER IS COMING

        A friend suggested that I write on this
subject. He remembers with consternation that
some friends of his were instructed by an "expert"
to cover their peonies with black plastic - and
lost them all.
        Winter losses of established plants that
are considered hardy for this area are due to
several causes. They include drying out, heaving
out of the ground due to repeated freezing and
thawing, rotting from dampness, too tender growth
brought on by late fertilizing with high nitrogen
fertilizers, wind damage, not tapering off on the
watering program so as to harden plants (the
woody ones), and believe it or not, too much protection.
        Let's start with the drying-out losses.

Many people do not realize that plants need some
moisture even in winter. During long dry spells,
the winter winds take their toll of moisture and
the dry plant roots shrivel and die. This happens
first to the more shallow-rooted plants, and as
the dryness goes deeper into the earth, the longer
roots of roses and other types of plants suffer
also. Fortunately, during such dry spells there
are bound to be some relatively warm days. On
one of these, a good soaking should be given the
entire cultivated area, lawns and all. This should
be done during the early part of the day so the
moisture will have dried off the plants before
nightfall. I have two hoses that are never put
away. One is attached to a faucet in the front
yard, and the other is at the back of the house.
One of these has one of those faucets that close
off inside the house and it is not necessary to
close it off in winter. The other has a readily
accessible shut-off in the basement and it takes
only a minute to run downstairs and turn it on or
off. With these I am ready to water at any time
the weather permits and a dry spell seems immi-
nent. Rarely is it necessary to water more than
three or four times during the winter months.

Heaving is caused by alternate freezing
and thawing. If it is severe enough, it will lift
plants out of the ground tearing their roots and
causing casualties. This can be prevented by not
mulching until after the first severe cold spell that
freezes the ground about two or three inches deep.

If frozen ground is mulched well it will not
thaw out, will retain moisture needed by the roots,
and will keep the earth from repeated thawings
until spring when the earth becomes warm again.
DO NOT MULCH before the freeze. It will prevent the earth from freezing as it should, and
later harder freezes will cause damage anyway.
Mulches that pack harbor pests and bacteria, so
use a loose mulch which allows air circulation. I
use trimmings from my numerous junipers as they
allow the plants to breathe. Soon the wind will

cover them with winter's debris and the dormant plants will stay safe until next spring.

Rotting from dampness is caused to a great extent by water standing in depressed areas. Try to provide a channel for a run-off if you cannot prevent the situation otherwise. Don't allow leaves or debris that pack and hold moisture to collect in big drifts as this adds to the dampness problem.

For some reason or other, a number of gardeners are tempted to fertilize during the late summer. If a nitrogen fertilizer is used it will stimulate new growth that will become very evident in six weeks or so. The tender new growth will fall victim to the first hard frost and damage to woody plants can be very severe. Don't use nitrogen after the middle of July. Instead a feeding of 0-10-10 or 0-20-0 fertilizer that strengthens the roots will be beneficial. Remember, your plants want to go to sleep, not to eat.

Winter damage can be especially severe where evergreens are concerned. The branches, heavily laden with snow, bend low and a sudden gust of wind can cause them to snap. To prevent this, tie rope around the tree or shrub in several places. If you feel that you must wrap your evergreens, use burlap or a strong cotton mesh. Do not use plastic film as protection as it will cut off air circulation and the sun will burn your plants through it. I do not wrap mine, but use roping to keep them from collapsing in the heavy snow. They weather the winter quite well, and if I should find a broken branch or two, removal of these is part of the spring pruning that keeps them within bounds.

Woody shrubs, (especially rosebushes) need hardening as cold weather approaches. This is done by curtailing watering - not the quantity, but the frequency of this chore. In late August, I start spacing watering days farther apart. As cool weather progresses, the rosebushes, the wisteria, flowering quinces, lilacs, forsythias and other woody plants find their waterings fewer and farther between. Roots reach for the farthest drops of subsurface water and in so doing give the plants a firmer anchor in the soil.

Too much protection can cause casualties. Remember that the more protection you give a plant, the more tender it will be and the harder the adjustment when protection is removed. A young tree carefully wrapped in paper is in much more danger of damage when unwrapped than one that has been loosely wrapped in burlap, or with a burlap shelter secured around it on poles so that the tree is not enclosed too tightly. Certain shrubs like rhododendrons and laurel cannot tolerate much wind, and a burlap screen is beneficial.

Plastic sheeting as a protection is a No-No. It stores too much heat on sunny days and will damage the parts of plants that it touches. Besides, it keeps the plant too warm during dormancy.

One year I mulched with wheat straw - I shall never forget that. All the wheat kernels in the straw fell to the ground. Field mice visited all winter long and in the spring the kernels they had missed caused a sizeable wheat crop to grow in the flower beds. If you can get straw, be sure there are no wheat kernels in it.

Peonies and iris need no winter protection. They need the winter's cold to make them bloom, and the iris needs the heat of the sun on its lightly covered rhizomes for the same reason.

ANTI-DESICCANT SPRAYS HELP EVERGREENS THROUGH WINTER

PREVENT MILDEW ON ROSES

Powdery mildew is one of the several woes that rose growers dread. The fine dust-like-covering on the leaves and their curled and twisted edges cause the gardener to run for the fungicide. Unfortunately, to date, fungicides are better preventives than cures.

In order to have a mildew-free garden, one should spray before the problem is evident.

Plants are not all mildew-prone to the same degree. Not only are different plants prone to various degrees, but plants in the same family show marked differences in their susceptibility to the problem. For instance, some roses are more easily attacked that others. Often one will find a rosebush with badly deformed, white-dusted leaves next to one or more that show no traces or very few of mildew.

There are several well-known fungicides on the market. Benlate is a systemic type and quite effective if used before signs of mildew are present. Funginex is recommended by the American Rose Society. Besides being quite effective, it is the least toxic of the well-known brands. A comparatively new one, Bayleton, has reported good results, but I have heard from well-known rosarians in the Bay Area that it has caused stem shortening, probably due to its greater toxicity.

We've all been using fungicides long enough to know the basic rules for obtaining the best results with the least phytotoxicity to the rosebushes and harm to the person spraying.

Now a new discovery has been found, something not planned for roses but intended to prevent drying out of evergreens, whether they be cut specimens for Christmas trees or the living evergreens-broadleaf and needleleafed types in our gardens. This product, an anti-desiccant (also known as anti-transpirant) spray has as its prime purpose the prevention of drying out of moisture from evergreens during the winter when gardens are not being watered as usual and drying winds wreak damage to the weakened plantings.

One or more of these better known products are on the market and obtainable at better garden shops everywhere. The names of the ones listed in the American Rose Society Magazine are Wilt-Pruf, Cloud Cover and Vapor Guard. These products leave a thin film of emulsified organic concentrate on the leaves of plants to which they are applied. They retard the loss of moisture and maintain the foliage in a healthy state.

The film coating at the same time prevents outside moisture from getting to the cell structure of the leaves and in doing so prevents the fungus from attacking the plant.

Since fungus needs moisture to grow, this step is useful in preventing it. Also, this coating protects tender new growth from drying winds that would damage it to a greater degree than it does older growth.

Most rosarians who have used these substances agree that a concentration of three or four teaspoons to a gallon of water make a good, working solution. Gardeners who do not exhibit their roses or who are not offended by the appearance of the residue have reported using as much as one ounce to a gallon and have found it very effective.

As to how often to spray – there seems to be no set agreement. Some would say that it may be used as often as once a week, while others say that periods up to almost a month are adequate. No doubt, the amount of rainfall in different areas accounts for the difference in opinions. One thing on which all agree – not to spray during the heat of the day or in windy weather.

Rosarians who have tried an anti-desiccant alone or in conjunction with a fungicide, seem to agree that even when used alone the former is effective as a mildew preventive. All stress that it should be used for best results as are the fungicides – to prevent mildew. It is not effective as a cure.

So apply anti-desiccants to your evergreens to help them through the winter – following directions on the container to the letter – and next growing season use them to prevent mildew on roses.

21. GARDEN CATALOGS FOR WINTER READING

Armchair gardening is one of the easiest
of tasks. No special clothing, no tools, no dirty
hands, no sore knees and no biting winds or hot
sun to make the task unpleasant. All you need is
a number of seed and plant catalogs and several
good gardening books and encyclopedias. Why
the latter? Most gardening catalogs are quite de-
pendable and make every effort to insure success
for their customers. They give a good description
of the plants, list the botanical names, and attempt
to give an idea of the relative hardiness of the
material offered for your garden.

I particularly like one of the catalogs
which I have been receiving for years. Although
I order very little as I am quite well supplied with
plants, I recommend it to new gardeners. It gives
common and botanical names for the plants listed.
In the case of trees a chart shows the height in
feet of the mature tree, the shape of the tree, and
gives the viewer an idea about how much area the
mature tree will shade. A zone map clearly marks
the temperature areas of the entire United States,
and the statement "-hardy through zone 5" leaves
no doubt as to whether the plant will survive in
our locale. Often I refer to this catalog in preparing articles for my column.

Several other catalogs do not give such
detailed information concerning zones and other
such pertinent data, but do give the botanical
names of their plants. In cases such as this it is
easy enough to refer to one of your gardening
books or encyclopedias, or even to the first catalog mentioned for the knowledge you seek.

Two beautiful bulb books can provide many
evenings of pleasant reading and "garden-wishing".
One is devoted almost entirely to spring blooming

bulbs, and the different types run into the hundreds. There are not too many pictures, but
those it has are clear and the colors very true.
I have also found the descriptions to be very accu-
rate. The other one deals with many different
kinds of bulbs and is full of illustrations. I have
bought several unusual bulbs from this firm and
they have proved to be all that was claimed for
them. Someone asked me upon looking at my copy,
"Do they really look like that, or is that picture
just something to get you to order them?" Yes,
if they are planted according to instructions, and
you will take a little time to read of these unusual
plants in your reference books, you will find that
they really look like that.

Now for a few pitfalls which may cause
the gardener some disappointment. The statement
"fastest growing of all oaks" is true. But, how
fast does an oak grow compared to a sycamore, a
mulberry, a birch or a maple? The description of
a fruit tree states ". . . will produce three bush-
els of fruit at maturity." That's wonderful isn't
it? But will that tree stand our climate? When
will it reach maturity? Will it blossom at such a
time that frosts will not damage it?

A statement such as the following is true
when a certain catalog deals with the east coast
– "will survive winters as far north as Washing-
ton, D.C., or Philadelphia, or Trenton, New Jersey." Quickly you run your finger across the
map following the latitude line and find that we
are in the same general position. But there are a
few other things to consider. All those places
mentioned are very near sea level. We are almost
a mile above. Their temperatures do not vary as
much as ours during a twenty-four hour period.
They are in a humid location. Ours is extremely
dry. This is the time for you to use your reference books. They will prove invaluable when the
location of the seed or plant company is in an
area so different from ours.

A seed catalog from the eastern coast is

one of my favorite wish books. Although it deals almost exclusively in seeds, the illustrations are lovely. The firm keeps up with all the newest plants and their material is excellent. I use this catalog a great deal as a reference book in selecting new bedding plants as I do not have time to raise too many from seeds. However, once in a while there is one kind I can't find on the market and then I send in an order for a packet or so of seeds and wait anxiously for them to arrive.

I should like to tell you to beware of the catalog that promises umpteen thousand blooms on one plant, a great splash of color and so forth, but neglects to give you the botanical name of the plant. Nine times out of ten you will be disappointed in one way or another.

Again, let me remind you that winter is the time for planning next year's activities in the yard. Get all the garden magazines and catalogs you can. Become acquainted with new plants, their habits, their ability to tolerate our climate, especially our extreme changes in temperature. Although I buy locally whenever possible, I subscribe to several garden magazines, order all kinds of catalogs using the coupons found in the magazines, and spend ample time studying them. Thus, when I see a new plant at a nursery, I am usually acquainted with its habits and do not have to take too long to decide if I want it, or if it will find a suitable place in my garden. You will find armchair gardening so easy and satisfying.

22. AT LAST—THE SECRET OF SUCCESS

Another year has gone and many gardening hours are behind you. I hope they have been successful and that you have learned many things. Most of all, I hope that your successes have fired you with enthusiasm and that you are getting ready for a better season next year.

Don't expect success in everything overnight – it won't come that way. However, if you will try to observe the following rules, there is no reason why you should not accomplish a great deal.

I have often, half-jokingly told visitors that I obtain success with my plants by threatening them with extinction if they do not start performing as they should. There is a method to this system and it does work most of the time. If you will follow the rules given, you too will attain your goals.

- Make sure you have duplicated or produced a reasonable substitute for the native environment if you have an indoor plant. For an outdoor plant use good judgment. Don't expect to raise tropicals or subtropicals here. Don't try to raise dry desert plants in an irrigated garden. In other words, don't try to cross Mother Nature.
- Make sure a plant is mature enough to produce flowers or fruit before giving up on it.
- Be sure you have the right soil mixture for it. Check the pH whenever possible. The Extension Service will help you here.
- Some houseplants or tub plants must become rootbound before they will bloom. Give them time to become so.
- Give plants sunshine, light and shade

according to directions from your
source of supply. They will do their
best to help you. After all, they are
in business to sell more plants.
- Some plants require a period of complete
rest between blooming cycles. If
they do not attain this through the
changes in the season, make it a
point to have them achieve it by
forcing it. It is especially necessary in houseplants.
- If the plant lives, but does not respond,
try a few experiments like changing
its location, varying the feeding substances and perhaps even changing
the soil.
- If after a reasonable time nothing happens,
go ahead and threaten. Be sure you
have a witness to your threat, and if
nothing happens in due time, carry out
your threat. Remember that someone
heard you make it, and you wouldn't
want to fall back on your word!

Did you put away all the garden tools except those few that will have to be used occasionally
during the winter? Now here's an embarrassing
question. Did you return all the tools and equipment you have borrowed over the growing season?
If not, it's time to do it now lest you fall victim to-

The Gardener's Curse

Oh, may slugworms and snails,
With their glutinous trails,
Flea beetles, thrips, ants
All beleaguer your plants.
May greenfly in billions
And mildew oppress
The roses you grow
With such hateful success.

May groundsel and sorrel
For precedence quarrel
And daisies like snow
On your tennis court grow.
May all your prime fruit trees
Be puckered with blight,
And moles on your lawn
Quarry deep through the night.

May mealybugs mangle
And strong vetches strangle,
May woodlice affright you
And centipedes bite you.
May earwigs attack you
And nest in your ears,
'Til you bring back my mower,
My roller, my shears!

A friend sent me this poem early one spring. I have read it over and over, and enjoy it more each time. Perhaps, that is because I have not borrowed anyone's garden tools.

If you have done so, why not clean them properly and return them to their rightful owners? Perhaps, then, they may let you borrow the wheelbarrow and that new hose next year.

APPENDIX I: PLANT LIST

This is a list of plants which I have grown at one time or another in my garden. All have done well on my south facing hillside location. Most should do well in this area with proper provisions for their care.

To insure success with all plantings one should observe the following points:

- be sure plant is suitable for climate zone
- select the right location considering sun and shade, wind direction, etc.
- provide the required soil conditions and adequate drainage
- mulch for protection if it is suggested

Because gardening is an all season job, follow up a good planting start with constant care.

ANNUALS

Aster *(Callistephus chinensis)*, white through lavender to scarlet - blooms from mid-summer into fall in full sun.

Baby's Breath *(Gypsophila elegans)*, white and pink flowers in mid-summer - full sun to partial shade

Bachelor's Button *(Centaurea cyanus)*, white, blue, pink and maroon blooms - from spring through fall in full sun (birds love the seeds).

Balsam *(Impatiens balsamina)*, white through red flowers from spring to fall in partial shade.

Bells of Ireland *(Moluccella laevis)*, pale green flowers in mid-summer to fall - in full sun.

Calendula *(Calendula officinalis)*, yellow through orange blooms from spring to fall in full sun.

ANNUALS

California Poppy *(Eschscholzia californica)*, yellow to deep orange - blooms in spring - full sun.

Candytuft *(Iberis amara)*, a border plant with white flowers from early spring to summer in full sun or partial shade.

Castor Bean *(Ricinus communis)*, white cluster of flowers in mid-summer in full sun (poisonous).

Cocks Comb *(Celosia)*, pink, red and gold flowers from mid-summer to fall in full sun.

Coleus *(Coleus hybridus)*, colorful foliage from summer to fall in partial shade.

Cosmos *(Cosmos bipinnatus)*, white through rose blooms from summer to fall in full sun.

Cranesbill *(Geranium)*, border plants with white through red flowers in summer - full sun.

Floss Flower *(Ageratum houstonianum)*, bedding plant with small clusters of blue blooms from summer through fall in full sun.

Flowering Kale *(Kale)*, vegetable with decorative foliage in summer - full sun.

(Gazania), yellow through red flowers from summer to fall in full to indirect sun.

Gentian Sage *(Salvia patens)*, dark blue flowers in summer - full sun or partial shade.

Impatiens *(Impatiens wallerana)*, white through red flowers from summer to fall in partial shade.

Johnny-Jump-Ups *(Viola tricolor)*, tiny purple and yellow pansy type flower from spring to fall in full sun to partial shade.

Larkspur *(Delphinium ajacis)*, white through pink and blue through red flowers in spring and summer in full sun.

ANNUALS

Lobelia *(Lobelia erinus)*, small flowers from light to dark blue from summer to fall in full sun.

Marigold *(Tagetes erecta)*, yellow through orange blossoms from spring through fall in full sun.

Moss Rose *(Portulaca grandiflora)*, a border plant or ground cover blooming in multi colors in summer – full sun.

Mullein Pink *(Lychnis coronaria)*, magenta to crimson flowers in spring and early summer – full sun to partial shade.

Nasturtium *(Tropaeolum)*, yellow through red blooms in spring through fall – full sun.

(Nicotiana), white through purple flowers from summer to fall in full sun to partial shade.

Painted Tongue *(Salpiglossis sinuata)*, pink through dark red blooms from summer to fall in full sun.

Petunia *(Petunia hybrida)*, multi color blooms from summer through fall in full sun.

Scarlet Sage *(Salvia splendens)*, white to red flowers from summer to fall in full sun to partial shade.

Snow on the Mountain *(Euphorbia marginata)*, foliage plant in summer – full sun or light shade.

Stock *(Matthiola)*, white through lavender flowers from summer to fall in full sun.

Sunflower *(Helianthus annuus)*, yellow blooms in summer – full sun.

Sweet Alysum *(Lobularia maritima)*, white to purple flowers from summer to fall in full sun to light shade.

Sweetpea *(Lathyrus odoratus)*, white to deep rose flowers from spring to summer in full sun.

ANNUALS

Verbena *(Verbena hortensis)*, white through red and blue flowers from summer to fall in full sun.

Zinnia *(Zinnia elegans)*, yellow through red and purple blooms from summer to fall in full sun.

BIENNIALS

Canterbury Bells *(Campanula medium)*, white through purple blossoms in summer – full sun or filtered shade.

Hollyhock *(Alcea rosea)*, wide range of colors in summer – full sun.

Money Plant *(Lunaria annua)*, lavender flowers in spring with shiny pods in fall – full sun to partial shade.

Oyster Plant *(Salsify)*, yellow or lavender flowers – sun – useful for dried arrangements.

Pansy *(Viola wittrockiana)*, wide range of colors and hybrids blooming from early spring to summer in partial to full shade.

Sweet William *(Dianthus barbatus)*, white through red flowers in spring and early summer in full sun to filtered shade.

BULBS (PERENNIAL)

(Allium), hybrids bloom from spring through summer in full sun – wide range of colors.

Arum *(Arum italicum)*, summer tuber with white flowers from summer to fall in partial shade.

(Brodiaea), corms with blue flowers in spring in full sun.

Calla *(Zantedeschia aethiopica)*, tender rhizome with white lily-like flowers in spring and summer in partial shade.

BULBS (PERENNIAL)

Camass *(Camassia esculenta)*, blue, white or yellow flowers in spring in full sun.

(Canna), tender tuberous rootstock with white through red blooms in summer – full sun.

(Crocus), corms with white, yellow or purple blooms in early spring – full sun.

Daffodil *(Narcissus)*, bulb with white through yellow flowers in early spring – full sun.

(Dahlia), tender tuberous rooted hybrids with blooms in a wide range of colors from spring into fall – full sun.

Day Lily *(Hemerocallis hybrids)*, tuberous rootstock with blooms in a wide range of colors in summer – full sun or light shade.

Dogtooth Violet *(Erythronium dens-canis)*, corms with flowers in white through violet colors in spring – full sun.

Four O'Clock *(Mirabilis jalapa)*, tuberous rootstock with red, yellow, or white blooms from mid summer through fall in full sun.

Fritillary *(Fritillaria imperialis)*, bulb with yellow through red blooms from late spring to early summer in full sun.

Gladiolus *(Gladiolus hortulanus)*, tender corm in a wide range of colors blooming from mid-summer through fall in full sun.

Glory of the Snow *(Chionodoxa)*, small bulb with tiny blue flower clusters in early spring in full sun.

Grape Hyacinth *(Muscari)*, small bulb with blue or white flower spike in early spring – full sun to light shade.

Guinea Hen Flower *(Fritillaria meleagris)*, bulb with a checkered red, brown and purple flower in late spring – full sun.

BULBS (PERENNIAL)

Hyacinth *(Hyacinthus orientalis)*, bulb with flowers in a wide range of colors in spring - full sun.

(Iris), rhizome with flowers in a wide range of colors - many hybrids - bloom from spring to early summer in full sun.

Jonquil *(Narcissus jonquilla)*, golden yellow flowers in spring - full sun to light shade.

Lily *(Lillium)*, bulbs with flowers in a wide range of colors - many hybrids - bloom in summer - full sun.

Lily of the Valley *(Convallaria majalis)*, pip with white, waxy, bell shaped fragrant flowers in spring - full sun to shade.

Meadow Saffron *(Colchicum autumnale)*, corm with lavender flowers in late summer to fall - full sun.

Montbretia *(Crocosmia crocosmiiflora)*, corm with orange-red flowers in spring - full sun to light shade.

Peruviana *(Scilla peruviana)*, small bulb with bluish purple, starlike flowers in late spring - filtered sun to light shade.

Siberian Squill *(Scilla siberica)*, small bulb with bright blue, tiny flowers in early spring - sun to light shade.

Snowdrop *(Galanthus)*, small bulb with bell shaped, nodding white flower in late winter to early spring - sun or partial shade.

Spring Star Flower *(Ipheion uniflorum)*, small bulb with white, star shaped flowers in spring - sun or partial shade.

Spuria *(Iris orientalis)*, rhizome with flowers of several colors in early summer - full sun.

BULBS (PERENNIAL)

Star of Bethlehem *(Ornithogalum umbellatum)*, small bulb with clusters of small white flowers in spring - sun.

(Triteleia), corm with blue and white flowers in spring and early summer - full sun.

Tuberous Begonia *(Begonia tuberhybrida)*, tender tuber with camellia-like flowers in white through orange and red from summer to fall - partial shade.

Tulips *(Tulipa)*, bulb with blooms in a wide range of colors and hybrids in spring - sun to partial shade.

Windflower *(Anemone)*, tuberous root with flowers in a wide variety of size and color from spring through fall in sun to light shade.

Winter Aconite *(Eranthis hyemalis)*, tuber with buttercup-like yellow flower in early spring - sun to partial shade.

Wood Hyacinths *(Endymion non-scriptus)*, flowers resembling hyacinths in varied colors in spring - sun to partial shade.

GROUND COVER & ROCK GARDEN PLANTS (PERENNIAL)

Aubrieta *(Aubrieta deltoidea)*, rock garden plant with tiny rose to purple flowers - early spring in full sun to partial shade.

Basket of Gold *(Alyssum saxatile)*, rock garden or border plant with golden yellow flowers - early spring in full sun or light shade.

Bishop's Weed *(Aegopodium podagraria)*, deciduous, invasive, ground cover - spring through fall in partial shade.

GROUND COVER & ROCK GARDEN PLANTS
(PERENNIAL)

Carpet Bugle *(Ajuga reptans)*, ground cover with
blue flowers – summer through fall in full sun
to partial shade.

Creeping Buttercup *(Ranunculus repens)*, invasive
ground cover with bright yellow button flowers
– spring to summer in filtered or deep shade.

Creeping Phlox *(Phlox subulata)*, ground cover
with flowers in wide range of colors – mid-
spring in full sun.

Hen and Chickens *(Sempervivum tectorum)*, evergreen rock garden plant – full sun or partial
shade.

Lamb's Ears *(Stachys byzantina)*, rock garden
plant with lavender flower stalks in summer –
full sun to light shade.

Money Wort *(Lysimachia nummularia)*, evergreen
ground cover with yellow flowers in summer –
shade.

Myrtle *(Vinca major)*, evergreen, invasive ground
cover with lavender flowers in spring – shade.

Plantain Lily *(Hosta decorata)*, ground cover with
lavender flowers in summer – semi sun through
shade.

Plumbago *(Ceratostigma plumbaginoides)*, ground
cover with blue flowers in summer – full
sun or light shade.

Rockcress *(Arabis caucasica)*, ground cover with
white flowers in early spring – full sun to
semi shade.

Sea Pink *(Armeria)*, evergreen ground cover with
white to pink flowers in spring – full sun.

Silver Spreader *(Artemisia caucasica)*, evergreen
ground cover in full sun.

GROUND COVER & ROCK GARDEN PLANTS (PERENNIAL)

Snow-in-Summer *(Cerastium tomentosum)*, ground cover with white flowers in early summer - full sun to light shade.

St. John's Wort *(Hypericum calycinum)*, invasive ground cover with yellow flowers - full sun to light shade.

Stonecrop *(Sedum)*, succulent ground cover in full sun to shade.

PERENNIALS

Anchusa *(Anchusa azurea)*, bright blue flower clusters from summer through fall in full sun - invasive.

Baby's Breath *(Gypsophila paniculata)*, tiny white flowers from summer through fall in full sun.

Bear's Breech *(Acanthus mollis)*, flower spikes from white to purple in spring to early summer - light shade.

Bee Balm *(Monarda didyma)*, white through scarlet flowers in summer - full sun to light shade.

Bell Flower *(Campanula glomerata)*, blue-purple bell shaped flower in early summer - full sun or light shade.

Bergenia *(Bergenia hybrids)*, border plant with pear tree rose to purple flowers in spring - partial shade.

Black-eyed Susan *(Rudbeckia hirta)*, yellow flowers with black centers from summer through fall in full sun.

Blanket Flower *(Gaillardia grandiflora)*, orange through red flowers from late spring through fall in full sun.

PERENNIALS

Bleeding Heart *(Dicentra spectabilis)*, rose-pink heart shaped flowers from late spring to early summer in partial shade.

Blue Flax *(Linum perenne)*, light blue flowers from spring through fall in full sun.

Candle Delphinium *(Delphinium elatum)*, flower spikes in wide range of colors from spring to summer in full sun.

Candytuft *(Iberis sempervirens)*, evergreen with white flowers from early spring to summer in full sun to partial shade.

(Cardoon), purple artichoke type flower in late summer - full sun.

Chinese Lantern *(Physalis alkekengi)*, invasive plant with white flowers that become papery orange lantern in summer - full sun or light shade.

(Chrysanthemum), flowers in wide range of colors - many hybrids from summer to late fall in full sun.

Columbine *(Aquilegia)*, delicate flowers in wide range of colors with many hybrids from spring to early summer - full sun.

Coneflower *(Echinacea purpurea)*, showy purple daisy-like flowers in summer - full sun.

Coral Bells *(Heuchera sanguinea)*, clusters of bell-shaped red or coral flowers from spring through fall in full sun or light shade.

Coreopsis *(Coreopsis grandiflora)*, bright yellow flowers from spring through fall in full sun.

Dusty Miller *(Senecio cineraria)*, textured gray-white leaves and clustered heads of cream or yellow flowers in summer - full sun.

Evening Primrose *(Oenothera berlandieri)*, rose pink flowers in summer - full sun.

PERENNIALS

False Dragonhead *(Physostegia virginiana)*, spike flowers of white to lavender in summer – full sun or partial shade.

Fleabane *(Erigeron)*, white to purple aster-like flowers from early summer to fall – full sun or light shade.

Forget-me-not *(Myosotis scorpioides)*, tiny blue flowers from spring through summer in partial shade.

Fox Glove *(Digitalis purpurea)*, biennial or perennial poisonous plant with purple-lavender splotched flowers in summer – partial shade.

Gas Plant *(Dictamnus alba)*, spike clusters of white flowers in summer – full sun or partial shade.

Gay Feather *(Liatris)*, fluffy, rosy-purple flower heads in summer – full sun.

Gloriosa Daisy *(Rudbeckia hirta)*, yellow, orange or russet flowers in summer – full sun.

Golden Glow *(Rudbeckia laciniata)*, growth to seven feet tall with bright yellow flowers in summer – full sun.

Gunnera *(Gunnera manicata)*, very large, corncob-like flower clusters in summer – partial shade.

Hibiscus *(H. moscheutos – palustris)*, large flowers in wide range of colors in summer – full sun – very large plant.

Iceland Poppy *(Papaver nudicaule)*, flowers in wide range of colors in summer – full sun.

Japanese Anemone *(Anemone hybrida)*, white to rose flowers in summer – partial shade.

Lavender *(Lavandula)*, lavender or purple flowers – used for sachets – summer in full sun.

Lupine *(Lupinus Russell hybrids)*, flowers in wide range of colors – spring to early summer in full sun.

PERENNIALS

Lythrum *(Lythrum salicaria)*, magenta colored flowers in summer to fall – full sun.

Maltese Cross *(Lychnis chalcedonica)*, scarlet flower clusters in early summer – full sun to light shade.

Marguerite *(Chrysanthemum frutescens)*, flowers in wide range of colors from spring to early summer in full sun.

(Mertensia), blue flowers resembling forget-me-not in spring to early summer – shade.

Mexican Primrose *(Clarkia amoena)*, pink or lavender flowers in spring to early summer – full sun.

Michaelmas Daisy *(Aster hybrid)*, flowers in white, pink, rose and purple in late summer to fall – full sun.

Monkshood *(Aconitum)*, blue flowers in summer – shade – very poisonous.

Oriental Poppy *(Papaver orientale)*, flowers in wide range of colors in late spring – full sun.

Painted Daisy *Chrysanthemum coccineum (pyrethrum roseum)*, pink, red and white flowers from mid-spring to summer in full sun.

Peony *(Paeonia)*, bloom in wide range of colors from mid-spring to early summer – full sun.

Phlox *(Phlox paniculata)*, white through rose and lavender flowers in summer – full sun.

Pincushion Flower *(Scabiosa columbaria)*, white through lavender flowers from mid-summer to fall – full sun.

Pinks *(Dianthus deltoides)*, rock garden plant with blooms white through deep pink in summer – full sun to light shade.

Primrose *(Primula polyanthus)*, blooms in wide range of colors from early spring to summer – shade.

PERENNIALS

Red Hot Poker *(Kniphofia uvaria)*, tall spikes of yellow through red flowers from spring through summer – full sun to partial shade.

Shasta Daisy *(Chrysanthemum maximum)*, white flowers from summer to fall in full sun to partial shade.

Snapdragon *(Antirrhinum majus)*, flowers in wide range of colors from spring to early summer – full sun.

Spider Wort *(Tradescantia andersoniana)*, white through purple and red flowers in summer – full sun or shade.

Speedwell *(Veronica hybrids)*, white, rose or blue flowers in mid-summer – full sun.

Stokes Aster *(Stokesia laevis)*, white through purple flowers from summer to early fall in full sun to light shade.

Violet *(Viola odorata)*, white to purple flowers in spring – partial shade.

Wild Sweetpea *(Lathyrus latifolius)*, lavender-pink flowers from spring to fall in full sun – invasive.

Yarrow *(Achillea millefolium)*, white, yellow or pink flower heads from summer to early fall in full sun or partial shade.

Yucca *(Yucca filamentosa)*, evergreen with bell-shaped white flowers on tall spikes in late spring – full sun.

SHRUBS

Azalea *(Rhododendron)*, Exbury and Mollis hybrids with white and yellow through red flowers in spring and early summer – shade.

Beauty Bush *(Kolkwitzia amabillis)*, deciduous with pink flower clusters in June – full sun.

SHRUBS

Blue Mist Spiraea *(Caryopteris clandonensis)*, deciduous with small blue flower clusters from mid-summer to fall in full sun.

Boxwood *(Buxus m. japonica)*, evergreen shrub in full sun or shade.

Bridal Wreath *(Spiraea prunifolia)*, deciduous with white flower clusters in mid-spring - sun or light shade.

Chaste Tree *(Vitex agnus-castus)*, lavender blue flower spikes from summer to fall in full sun.

Cinquefoil *(Potentilla fruticosa)*, small yellow flowers in spring and summer - full sun to partial shade.

Creeping Cotoneaster *(Cotoneaster adpressus)*, deciduous, low growing shrub with small white to pink flowers in spring - full sun.

Daphne *(Daphne odora)*, evergreen with very fragrant pink flower cluster in early spring - full sun to partial shade - needs protection.

Firethorn *(Pyracantha)*, evergreen with white flower clusters in spring and orange or red berries in fall - full sun.

Flowering Almond *(Prunus triloba)*, deciduous with pink or white flowers in spring - full sun.

Flowering Quince *(Chaenomeles)*, deciduous with white, pink and red flowers in early spring - full sun - many species.

Forsythia *(Forsythia suspensa)*, deciduous with yellow flowers in early spring - full sun.

Fragrant Sumac *(Rhus aromatica)*, deciduous with tiny yellow flowers in summer - full sun to partial shade.

Gold Dust Plant *(Aucuba japonica)*, evergreen, dark green leaves spotted with yellow - shade.

156

SHRUBS

Holly *(Ilex)*, evergreen - part sun or shade.

Hydrangea *(Hydrangea arborescens, H. quercifolia, H. paniculata)*, deciduous with large white flower clusters in summer and fall - partial shade - needs protected area.

Juniper *(Juniperus)*, evergreen - full sun or semi shade.

Laurel *(Laurus nobilis)*, evergreen with small yellow flowers in spring - partial shade.

Lilac *(Syringa vulgaris)*, deciduous with white to purple flower clusters in mid-spring - full sun.

Magnolia *(Magnolia soulangiana)*, deciduous with pink and white tulip-shaped flowers in mid-spring - full sun - avoid wind.

Mock Orange *(Philadelphus)*, deciduous with fragrant white flowers in late spring - full sun to partial shade.

Oregon Grape *(Mahonia aquifolium)*, evergreen with yellow flower clusters in spring - full sun to partial shade.

Photinia *(Photinia fraseri)*, evergreen with white flower clusters in spring - full sun or semi shade.

(Rhododendron), evergreen hybrids with flowers in wide range of colors from mid to late spring in filtered shade.

Rose *(Rosa)*, deciduous with flowers in wide range of colors - many hybrids - blooms from spring through fall in full sun.

Rose of Sharon *(Hibiscus syriacus)*, deciduous with pink, white or lavender flowers from mid-summer to fall in full sun to partial shade.

Scotch Broom *(Cytisus scoparius)*, evergreen with yellow through red flowers in late spring - full sun.

SHRUBS

Snowball *(Viburnum opulus "Roseum")*, deciduous with white flower cluster resembling snowball in spring – full sun.

Snowberry *(Symphoricarpos albus)*, deciduous with white flower clusters in spring – white berry fruit attractive to birds in fall – full sun or semi shade.

Tree Peony *(Paeonia suffruticosa)*, deciduous with large pink through purple flowers in mid-spring – full sun to partial shade.

(Weigela), deciduous with pink to rose flowers in mid-spring – full sun to partial shade – many species.

Winter Jasmine *(Jasminum nudiflorum)*, deciduous and viny with small yellow flowers in late winter – full sun or partial shade.

Yellow Grove Bamboo *(Phyllostachys aureosulcata)*, full sun or semi shade.

TREES

Black Locust *(Robinia pseudoacacia)*, deciduous – fast growing – fragrant white flower clusters in spring – brittle branches apt to snap in wind.

Candle Tree *(Catalpa speciosa)*, deciduous with large upright clusters of white flowers in spring.

Crabapple *(Malus)*, deciduous with white through pink flowers in spring.

Dogwood *(Cornus)*, deciduous with white through deep pink flowers in spring.

Floss Silk Tree *(Albizia julibrissin)*, deciduous and fast growing with pink fluffy flowers in summer.

TREES

Flowering Cherry *(Prunus)*, deciduous with pink flowers in spring.

Flowering Peach *(Prunus)*, deciduous with white through deep pink flowers in spring.

Flowering Plum *(Prunus)*, deciduous with white to pink flowers in spring.

Golden Chain Tree *(Laburnum anagyroides)*, yellow hanging flower clusters in spring - poisonous seed pods.

Goldenrain Tree *(Koelreuteria paniculata)*, deciduous and slow growing with small yellow flower clusters in summer.

Hawthorn *(Crataegus)*, deciduous with red or white flowers in spring and red berries in fall.

Kwanzan Cherry *(Prunus serrulata)*, deciduous with deep pink flowers in spring.

Mountain Ash *(Sorbus)*, deciduous with clustered white flowers in spring and orange to red berries in fall.

Redbud *(Cercis occidentalis)*, deciduous small tree with magenta flowers in spring.

Rose Acacia *(Robina hispida)*, deciduous with deep rose flower clusters in spring.

Smoke Tree *(Cotinus coggygria)*, deciduous with puffs of purple to lavender flowers.

Tulip Tree *(Liriodendron tulipifera)*, deciduous with greenish-yellow tulip shaped flowers in late spring.

Weeping Cherry *(Prunus)*, deciduous with small, pink flowers on 'weeping' branches in spring.

Weeping Peach *(Prunus)* deciduous with deep pink flowers on 'weeping' branches in spring.

VINES

Boston Ivy *(Parthenocissus tricuspidata)*, semi-evergreen or deciduous vine.

(Clematis), deciduous with flowers in wide range of colors in spring - full sun.

Honeysuckle *(Lonicera)*, evergreen or deciduous with white and yellow nectared flowers in spring - full sun.

Morning Glory *(Ipomoea)*, perennial or annual with blue, pink or white flowers from spring through fall in full sun.

Silver Lace Vine *(Polygonum auberti)*, deciduous with small white flowers in frothy mass from spring to fall in full sun.

Trumpet Vine *(Campsis radicans)*, deciduous with orange flowers from summer to fall - full sun.

Virginia Creeper *(Parthenocissus quinquefolia)*, deciduous with red leaves in fall - full sun or shade - very invasive.

Wisteria *(Wisteria sinensis)*, deciduous with long lavender flower clusters in spring - full sun or light shade.

APPENDIX II: RECOMMENDED CATALOGS

Bluestone Perennials – 7211 Middle Ridge Road
Madison, Ohio   44057   (perennials)

Breck's – P. O. Box 1757 – Peoria, Illinois   61656
(bulbs)

W. Atlee Burpee Co.   – 300 Park Ave. – Warmin-
ster, Pennsylvania   18974   (seeds, supplies)

Cooley's Gardens – P. O. Box 126 – Silverton,
Oregon   97381   (iris – cat. $2.00)

Henry Field Seed & Nursery Co. – 407 Sycamore
Street – Shenandoa, Iowa   51602   ($10.00 min.)

Guerney Seed & Nursery Co. – 2nd & Capital
Yankton, South Dakota   57078

Huff's Garden Mums – P. O. Box 187 – Burlington,
Kansas   66839   ($5.00 min.)

Jackson & Perkins – P. O. Box 1028 – Medford,
Oregon   97501   (roses and other plants)

Nor' East Miniature Roses – 58 Hammond Street
Rowley, Massachusetts   01969   ($6.00 min.)

Park Seed Co., Inc. – P. O. Box 46 – North Green-
wood, South Carolina   29648

Rancho de la Flor de Lis – P. O. Box 227
Cerrillos, New Mexico   87010   (iris – cat. $1.00)

Rosehill Farm – Greg Neck Road – Galena, Maryland
21635   ($20.00 min.)

Roses by Fred Edmunds – 6235 W. Kahle Road
Silsonville, Oregon   97070

Roses of Yesterday and Today – 805 Brown's Valley
Road – Watsonville, California   95076
(cat. $2.00)

Schreiner's Gardens – 3625 Quinaby Road, N.E.
  Salem, Oregon 97303 (iris – cat. $2.00)

Sequoia Nursery – 2519 E. Noble Ave. – Visalia,
  California 93277   (Moore Miniature Roses)

Stocking Rose Nurseries – 785 N. Capitol Ave.
  San Jose, California 95133

Sunnyslope Gardens – 8638 Huntington Drive
  San Gabriel, California 91775
  (chrysanthemums)

Thompson & Morgan – P. O. Box 1308 – Jackson,
  New Jersey 08527   (seeds)

Ty Ty Plantation – P. O. Box 159 – Ty Ty,
  Georgia 31795   (bulbs – $5.00 min.)

Van Ness Water Gardens – 2460 N. Euclid – Upland,
  California 91786   (cat. $2.00 – $15.00 min.)

Wayside Gardens – P. O. Box 1 – Hodges,
  South Carolina 29695   (some of everything –
  cat. $1.00)

INDEX